SIR AND MISS ANNIE

For Suzi + Jed

SIR AND MISS ANNIE

with love

Alice Tipton LaFleur

[signature]

LAKE OGLETHORPE PRESS

For my children Sara Jane and Tipton,
my sister Catharine,
my husband Rick,
and of course for Sir and Miss Annie—
with love

CONTENTS

PART THREE: The War Years

FOREWORD

"Sir" and "Miss Annie" were my wife Alice's parents, Jim (General James Baird) Tipton, raised in the small Missouri town of Senath, and Ann Livingston Little, of Rochester, New York. Their fathers were both doctors, but the two men were entirely unalike in temperament. Their moms were quite different too, one a strong-minded southern lady, the other an independent-minded artist. Ann and Jim's upbringing could not have been more dissimilar, nor their ultimate romance and marriage more unlikely.

Alice begins *Sir and Miss Annie* with a fascinating account of her parents' family backgrounds. The second part of the book provides a gallery of compelling, often charming glimpses into their childhoods, youth, and schooling, including Ann's travels in Europe and Jim's years studying aeronautical engineering and playing football on scholarship for the University of Alabama's powerhouse team.

But the heart of Alice's narrative is the story of how Ann and Jim's paths crossed in Europe during WW2, where he served as a fighter pilot and group commander and she as a Red Cross volunteer.

I never met Sir at all and I knew Miss Annie for only a year and a half, from when I first met Alice in February, 2003, until her mom's death in August, 2004. And yet I feel that in many ways I know both of my wife's parents better than I knew my own. Alice, her children Sara and Tip, and her older sister Catharine ("Cat") all deeply cherished Sir and Miss Annie; so even did friends and neighbors on Lake Oglethorpe, where the two of them lived for several years in the lakefront cabin Alice designed for them and where, after Sir's death, Ann lived in a gracious suite in Alice's home (also of her design).

So from the time Alice and I got together, I had abundant opportunity to hear stories about her mom and dad, their meeting in WW2, and their experiences with Alice and Cat in Japan, Korea, Turkey, and numerous stateside bases where Sir, who rose ultimately to the rank of Major General, was assigned increasingly responsible military commands. There were lots of stories too, nearly all of them happy, about their retirement years and the love and support they showered upon their two daughters and their grandchildren Tip and Sara.

I used to tell my children and friends that one big reason I married Alice (there were many!) was her mom. Folks say, if you're thinking of taking a bride, consider her mother — as that's who she'll turn into. Not a bad deal, I thought, as Annie was nothing but grace, passion, intelligence, determination, and goodness. And these are traits she did indeed pass on to her younger daughter. Alice is Miss Annie in so many ways, but she is her dad as well, as I have discovered over our 14 years together. Besides his steely blue eyes and startling good looks, she inherited Sir's industriousness, his persistence, and his modesty. Sir passed on his mechanical aptitude too, I might add, as Alice is our household carpenter, electrician, plumber, painter, landscaper, and jack-of-all-trades.

Another talent of Alice's that she inherited from both parents is her skill at writing. Miss Annie was a bit more of a natural, as her abiding interest in French was an indication of her aptitude for language in general. She was an avid journaler, and her diaries, annotated calendars, and copious personal correspondence were invaluable resources for this book. Sir was not so much a literary sort, but when called upon to chronicle his USAF service, particularly in WW2, he rose to the task, as he did to all other responsibilities in his life. An 85-page memoir he wrote out by hand in 1982 for a friend who had asked about his recollections from the war, and the "Oral History" he provided the Air Force in 1985 both reveal his knack for story-telling.

Alice never considered herself a writer at all, until, with a bit of encouragement from an admiring husband who considered her capable of nearly every kind of achievement, she audited a couple of creative writing classes at the University of Georgia (where she had worked for several years in institutional research and planning, and where I was still employed as a professor of classical languages). Her essays and short stories were beyond anything either of us had imagined she might do, and her poetry was likewise remarkably good. When I began reading her work, I realized I should not have been surprised. She brought the same meticulous aesthetic and sense of structure and proportion to her writing that she had summoned in designing our home, her previous house, and her parents' Lake Oglethorpe cabin.

To write well, one must first read a lot, and Alice has always been an avid reader. I can't remember a day in our lives together when she has not had a book at hand, and dived into reading, especially at bedtime (during the daytime hours she's always too busy in her gardens, or decorating and redecorating the houses, to make our little world more beautiful, or sewing, or repairing or remodeling things to make our world more functional). Reading by itself, however, won't make a writer. The classes certainly helped (thank you, Professors Kyle Garrett and especially Ida Stewart), so there's the "nurture" part. But the inheritance from Sir and Miss Annie, the "nature" part, was certainly the principal factor in bringing this book into being. The passion and perseverance and innate interest in language (a reason, I like to think, that she married a Latin professor!) Alice inherited from her mom, and the orderliness, and resolve, and get-it-done attitude she learned from the General, are all ingrained in the soul and substance of this book. The trove of diaries, memoirs, and letters written by both her parents, and dutifully preserved and stored away by her mom were Alice's invaluable primary sources; occasional gaps are filled in here and there with a bit of creative fiction inspired by her fond memories of life with Miss Annie and Sir, the Red Cross girl and the flyboy.

Rick LaFleur

PREFACE

Every love story is uncommon. My older sister Catharine would frequently ask our parents, Ann Little and Jim Tipton, for their story of "the Red Cross girl and the flyboy," telling of how they met. It was a complicated tale. Once, in an attempt to get the facts straight, we videotaped them on their 46th anniversary as we urged them to reminisce about falling in love during WW2, but the exchange was the typical confusion of partial memories and constant interruptions, as they tried to piece it all together without revealing too much.

After our parents died, I decided to organize their jumble of memorabilia, tucked away in boxes and trunks in our two attics. There was enough to fill a storage unit. I felt sure it would all get tossed out if I didn't pare it down into a manageable size for my children, Sara and Tip, who would inherit everything someday. In the process I came upon a series of unread letters my mother had written for Sara shortly after she was born in 1984. It seems the letters had been intentionally secreted away, waiting to be found later when Sara was older. They read like a memoir and chronicle much of my mother's life as a child and young woman.

I already possessed the diary mother kept and letters she posted during WW2, plus a transcription of an interview, given by my father, which documented his memories of serving in the military. But there was also a memoir he had written for a colleague, reading like a stream of personal musings on WW2. As I examined each saved treasure, I became convinced I should add my parents' unique adventures to the many WW2 love stories from all over the world.

I decided to title the book *Sir and Miss Annie,* their pet names for each other and the names my children remember them by. "Miss Annie" is obvious, a southern boy's endearment for his sweetheart. "Sir" became my father's name when my sister was reintroduced to him after he had been away, fighting in the Korean War, for what seemed to her a very long time. He called my sister "Kit," a double entendre for "Catharine" and "kitten," and she adored him. She was only three and coquettishly called him "Sirsy" as she curled up in his lap. It was her interpretation of the proper use of manners with a daddy she'd been missing. From then on it was "Sir" and "Miss Annie," and I never heard my mother call my father by any other name.

Objectively, it would seem that my parents came from nearly identical backgrounds. Both families sailed to North America in the first wave of immigrants to the New World. Both were raised by physician fathers with much younger wives, and both had the benefit of a post-secondary education. But the memories passed down on the Littles' side, whose descendants arrived on the Mayflower in 1620, and the benchmark tales of the Tiptons, who arrived 40 years later on the S.S. Friendship, couldn't have been more unalike.

I grew up knowing about my mother's spooky old house and my father's line of strong, blue-eyed kinfolk, but it wasn't until I began cataloging and researching those and other heirloom anecdotes, that I truly understood how long the odds were against these two finding each other, much less falling in love. It was as though they had grown up on alien worlds, circling the same sun. I have tried in this book to capture that very WW2 legacy, when our American "melting pot" of people came together under one sky, as embodied by my parents – Sir and Miss Annie.

Here I must give thanks to the community of friends and family that supported my efforts to create this book: first to my children Sara and Tip, as they are the reason for this project; to my sister Catharine, for her inspired and romantic heart; to my Tipton cousins, Rick, Pat and Joe (Moody) and my Little cousins, Skip, Henry, Farley (Barbera), Zeke, Nick and Johnny (both Phillips), who all provided choice insider details on our family and shared photographs with me; to my readers Jackie Cabe, Susan Dorsey, Chris Halderson, Suzanne Kelly, and Lois Swoboda, for giving me feedback and keeping me focused; to genealogy aficionados Bob Curtis, John Parrish, Tony Byrd, and Bert Lok for helping me get the facts straight; to the picture gurus Pam and Bruce Barker, who rescued some precious old photographs using the latest technology; to Matthew Frye, of the Tipton-Haynes State Historic Site, and Alicia Phelps, of the Northeast Tennessee Tourism Association, who assisted with photos and information on the Tipton-Haynes House; to Kay Stanton, who masterfully executed and improved upon the design I had envisioned for both cover and interior; last to my husband Rick, who lovingly rendered all of the above services in addition to being my editor and patient encourager-in-chief while I struggled to be worthy of the story I was telling.

Alice Tipton LaFleur
Summer, 2017
Lake Oglethorpe

INTRODUCTION

The unlikely account of how Ann Livingston Little and James Baird Tipton became a duo is one worth telling. When the U.S. jumped into WW2 on December 7, 1941 (the "day of infamy"), Ann had just turned 27 the month before, while Jim wouldn't be 27 until two months later. The family joke always figured mother as an "older woman," stalking my father all over Europe during the war, until he finally gave up and surrendered. That was his style of humor, with mother typically raising an eyebrow to give him that knowing look whenever he willingly perpetuated this ironic misinformation.

As a lifelong "joiner," my gregarious mother was a member in and sustainer of many clubs, most notably the Twigs of Rochester, New York, the Junior League, the Alliance Française and the Daughters of the American Revolution, plus various opera guilds, bridge groups and charitable organizations, and she would always sign up for the thrift-shop detail in whichever Episcopal Church she was then attending. She was from urban upstate New York, the baby of four, pragmatic and a versatile communicator.

My father was more of a self-conscious maverick and not too interested in social clubs, but he still enjoyed organized affiliations. He attained the grade of Eagle Scout as a youth, was awarded a Sports Illustrated Silver All America Award for college football and retired a Major General in the United States Air Force. Despite his ambivalence towards people, he still had a quality that enabled him to be a leader of men. He was from rural, small-town Missouri, the firstborn of two, idealistic and largely taciturn.

I was lucky to have legacy documents, pictures, newspaper clippings, magazine articles, resource books, letters, diaries, speeches, journals, transcriptions, scrapbooks and memoirs saved by my parents and later carefully stored away by my mother for me to find. She hoped I might develop an interest in our heritage, which I did. She had also assembled a genealogical tree, going back to the first arrival of the Littles and Tiptons in North America. So I begin this narrative early in each family's history in order to give context to Ann Little's and Jim Tipton's differing world views and spotlight how they may have regarded themselves in relation to each other when they first met. The story is fundamentally told in my father's and mother's own words: they "wrote" it through what they left behind, and I only supplied the mortar to give the elements an architecture and flow.

Ann Livingston Little, in her early 20s

James Baird Tipton, in his early 20s

PART ONE

EARLY FAMILY HISTORIES

Chapter 1

TIPTON ROOTS AND MISHAPS

"Little" is a common, ancient name. Widely employed, it could refer to a group of people small in stature, small in number, originating from a second son, or it could be a playful name for big people. In contrast, my father's surname "Tipton" seems to have come much later, since it is thought to be associated with a specific activity and place. By this theory, it is a variant of a name that refers to a distinct set of people who celebrated "St.Tibba" in mid-December during the early settlement of England. A village called Tibintone, or "Tibba's Town," is cataloged in Britain's Domesday Book of property holdings, ca. 1086.

In trying to document the origin of the name "Tibba," my husband found this quote in a book about Christian Saints:

> [Tibba] was, it is thought, a member of the ruling family of Mercia in the 7th century, perhaps a niece of King Penda.

Penda traced his lineage back to Wihtlæg, the mortal offspring of the Nordic god Odin. Early on, the "old ways" were still being observed in many parts of his kingdom, Anglo-Saxon Mercia, situated in the Midlands of England. His relative, a solitary nun named Tibba, was widely known in this region for her skill in falconry and game-hunting, much like the Greco-Roman goddess Artemis or Diana. Due to Tibba's connection to Odin, people who knew of her considered her divine and superstitiously believed that petitioning her could help them bring down prey.

After her death she was canonized for her exemplary life as a Christian, but St. Tibba's many adherents continued to believe their very survival depended on her blessings. Though it was possible for the gods to beget human children in polytheistic religions, this didn't jibe with the quickly rising faith of the "Father, Son and Holy Ghost," which had reduced all deity into a trinity of one. Christianity was coming into its own and by then the conflation of Tibba the Saint and Tibba the Goddess was so entrenched in the ethos of those who prayed to her that it alarmed the monotheistic purists. Her name was ultimately expunged from early Christian texts in an effort to eradicate any hint of pagan influence. Tibba is obscurely remembered today, but only because her bones were preserved and enshrined as religious relics in Peterborough Abbey, in Cambridgeshire, England, possibly by a Tipton.

The Tiptons may have gotten their first superstar in a story set in the 11th century when a deciding battle ended in favor of King Edward I of England against rebels from Wales. In this widely disputed version of history, victory was won when a Scotsman from Shropshire, riding a charger in full armor, pursued a lone Welshman fleeing on horseback into the surrounding woods beneath Snowdon Mountain. The rider turned to duel in knightly combat, but he was toppled from his horse after being struck dead by our forebear, Anthony Tipton. When searching his opponent's coat of mail for valuables, Anthony discovered he had killed the Welsh leader, the most wanted man in the British realm. In this Tipton version of history it was our ancestor that had destined Llewelyn to become the last Prince of Wales.

According to this tradition, Anthony guarded the dead prince where he dropped, until Llewelyn could be identified and his head hacked off and taken to be pilloried by King Edward on his castle wall. Edward I, also known as the "Hammer of the Scots" or "King Longshanks," was reportedly so delighted with his soldier that he knighted Anthony on the spot as "Sir Anthony de Tipton," giving us our coat of arms. It features swords and the motto *CAVSAM DECIDIT,* "He decided the cause."

The stories connecting our family surname both to the "divine" Saint Tibba and to the heroic warrior de Tipton continue to be passed down as Tipton family fact. The bold self-image may be what perpetuates them, since both legends are historically disputable, but it's an attractive notion to have a bloodline that includes a "Norse Goddess" and a "Royal Knight" in any family that takes itself seriously.

Tipton family crest, apparently invented by some 20th century entrepreneur

Chapter 2

THE COLONEL JOHN WARS

Some of my primary source-material for the Tipton clan came from two genealogies, *The Tipton Family*, by W. Hord Tipton (1948), and *We Tiptons and our Kin*, by Ervin Charles Tipton (1978). Both books are self-published, exhaustively researched, and may be difficult to endure if you are not one of "us," but the painstaking years the authors spent accumulating the materials set forth is impressive.

In *The Tipton Family,* Hord Tipton wrote:

> During the year of 1901 I had the pleasure of paying a visit to Mr. Thompson L. M. Tipton of Dunnville, Ontario, Canada who told me that the Maryland and Virginia Tiptons were the same Tiptons that descended from Sir Anthony de Tipton.

Whether there was ever a Sir Anthony de Tipton or not, the original Tipton immigrant to North America is convincingly identified as Edward Tipton, from Shropshire, England, of old Britannia. He was soon joined by his son, Jonathan, born in 1639.

Jonathan Tipton's obituary was published in the *Maryland Gazette*, January 27, 1757:

> We are informed that the beginning of this month, died Mr. Jonathan Tipton aged 118 years. He was born at Kingston on Jamaica, which place he left while young, and lived almost ever since in this Province, and had his perfect senses to the last, especially a remarkable strength of memory. His youngest sons are reconed [sic] among the oldest men in Baltimore County.

The lifespan of the man is reason enough to include him in this text – but the real snare is the whole memory thing. Every Tipton generated from this branch is haunted by the prospect of this potential DNA jackpot, wondering if their children might receive the genetic gift of such a retentive mind. I know this trait was manifested in toto at least once, seven generations later, in the person of my grandfather, Dr. Paul Light Tipton.

In the early documentation of the hard-living, hard-fighting, adventurous Tipton tribe, one particular man is a standout. He was a certain kind of man and the grandson of the above mentioned centenarian. His name was Colonel John Tipton (1730-1813), and he stood six feet tall and fathered nine sons by his first wife, Mary Butler. He was 21 when they were married in Baltimore, but soon moved south to Virginia and settled in what ultimately became known as Shenandoah County. A patrician, he was first a loyal British colonist and then became a loyal American patriot in the Revolutionary War of Independence.

Being at the right place at the right time, Colonel Tipton was there at the Williamsburg convention when Virginia declared its freedom from England and later had the opportunity to vote George Washington into office as our first president. He was civically minded and served Virginia as Court Justice, High Sheriff, and a member of the House of Burgesses, as well as being a vestryman for the Church of England. He was a dour, but well-respected planter with a reputation for raising fast horses.

At the mature age of 53, Colonel John Tipton decided to move closer to his father and two younger brothers on the other side of the Appalachians, in what was then part of North Carolina's territory. He built his last home, a two-story log cabin, near Sinking Creek, a tributary of the Watauga River. The site he chose was in a popular American Indian hunting ground near a famous tree that boasted an authentic Daniel Boone hand-carved message about a bear kill dated 1760. This move caused a ripple in our history, and his cabin is now preserved on the Tipton-Haynes State Historic Site in Tennessee; but the place could easily have become the hallowed ground of Frankland Nation.

Colonel John Tipton. No actual portrait has survived; sketch, by Jenny Kilgore, courtesy of John Parrish, who provided her with descriptions from historical texts.

Working together to gain independence from Britain, the original 13 colonies had begun the transition from individual nation states into a consortium of equals. Everything was in high flux, and the unification cause needed support in the way of funding. In less than a year after Colonel John built his new home, the current North Carolinian politicos offered their western territory to the new central government in payment for its share of the war debt. Congress decided it wasn't worth the effort to collect taxes from that underpopulated fringe of civilization, so they tabled the offer for "further consideration."

When this quid pro quo reached the far side of the mountains, the people living there felt insulted by their fellow North Carolinians and balked at the highhanded proposal. They decided to withdraw their affiliation from a colony that didn't value them and form an altogether new settlement they called Frankland (an early Anglo-Saxon placename meaning "free-land"). They created their own government and elected the firebrand militia commander of the "Overmountain Men," Colonel John Sevier, as their charismatic leader. He was well known for his part in the Battle of Kings Mountain, a decisive moment in the war for liberty, and was a very popular choice.

In the meantime, North Carolina had retracted its offer to collateralize the land. In short, the North Carolina Territory cession was rescinded even as its residents seceded. It was a true mess, but the prospect of a different, freer kind of republic was so compelling it gained traction and quickly grew into an aspirational Franklander movement, ranging from southwest Virginia all the way into Alabama. There were murky rumors of financial backing from Spain, whose leaders desired a firmer grip on the Americas. The fear of another country's involvement whipped up emotions in the new commonwealth and caused a lot of hard feelings. For almost five years secession remained the impassioned quest for many of the disenfranchised pioneers in the outer reaches of our heartland; but not for all.

During this time the name "Frankland" was changed to "Franklin," in deference to the famous statesmen Ben Franklin. He was a wary but respected supporter of the dissidents' libertarian ideals, and rebranding themselves by using his name seemed like a good strategy to gain legitimacy among those who weren't yet convinced. It didn't work. All proposals to deal with the raggedy split had gone unresolved, and the territory's settlers were exhausted with the competing factions. There was double taxation, poor law enforcement, worse record-keeping and nonexistent compromise between the North Carolina and the Franklander coalitions. Making matters worse, the Indian Wars continued to strain the scant resources available to the hold-outs on both sides. The situation was so unworkable it led to confusion, anarchy, finger-pointing and distrust between neighbors and within families. In the middle of it all were two defiant men...as unalike as any two men could be.

There was a series of altercations between Colonel John Tipton and Colonel John Sevier. Both were ex-militia men, once freedom fighters, who lived less than five miles apart and drank from the same river. Buried deep in America's western territories, they completely fell out over the status of their mutually beloved spot on earth. Oddly, their animosity mirrors the same tensions between state and federal parameters Americans still worry with today. While "to form a more perfect union" was being inked by the Constitutional Congress in Philadelphia, the Franklanders were furiously bent on becoming autonomous and tearing away from what they considered government overreach.

North America could have become a continent more like Europe, with multiple countries instead of a network of States, but Colonel John Tipton didn't side with the upstarts and held firmly to the federalist ideology. He wanted his territory to stay whole and give up the "freeland" vision. He paid for his stance with ridicule. He took the brunt of the separatists' frustration and his detractors nicknamed him "Severe John" in mock comparison to their own political darling, John Sevier, a scrappy man who really knew how to work a crowd.

Here's one version of the "Battle of the State of Franklin," as narrated by genealogist Hord Tipton in his book, *The Tipton Family:*

> In 1788, strained relations between Governor John Sevier and Colonel John Tipton had reached a point that when they finally met on the street they decided to settle their differences in the old fashioned way; it is said that Colonel Tipton was a powerful man and was soon the victor over his old enemy.

> Afterward, Governor Sevier started to the home of Colonel Tipton with some of the [Franklin] state troops under his control; he reached the neighborhood of Colonel Tipton's house early in the morning and ordered Tipton to surrender.

> Tipton had about forty-five of his friends and neighbors congregated in his house to help him.

> When Sevier sent word for him to surrender, he sent an answer "Hell No! In less than two hours you will be surrendering to me." He had sent for [North Carolina] reinforcements.

It could have been Sevier's victory, as he initially had more troops on site, but early in the morning, as the skirmish began, a thick white-out snow fell so fast it was impossible to see. This delay was a boon to Tipton and his backers, allowing Sevier's forces to be outnumbered by the North Carolina operatives when they arrived later that day. On February 29, leap year 1788, three men were dead, prisoners had been taken and the de facto end of the "Republic of Frankland" was accomplished.

Hord Tipton adds:

> During the battle one of Sevier's men was killed leaving a needy widow, and it is a well-known fact that Colonel Tipton out of the generosity of his heart gave a negro slave to the widow of the man killed.

Ha! That postscript gives a bizarre twist to the "shoot-out" at the Tipton home and becomes even more twisted when you know the slave "gifted" had, earlier that month, been confiscated from his political adversary, Colonel John Sevier, by the North Carolina militia and consequently "stored" in Colonel John Tipton's basement. This rendition leaves out much of the instructive political background, but the feral south – out of step, close to the bone and only half apologetic – still comes through in this blustery tale of two strong-willed men told by a later-day Tipton.

Nation building is never easy, but the real truth of the matter came to light when this contested territory was peacefully melded into the eastern portion of a new state called Tennessee – with John Sevier as governor for three terms and John Tipton as state senator for two. Tipton was drafted to co-write the Tennessee Constitution, which Thomas Jefferson later declared was "the least imperfect and most republican of any system of government adopted by any of the American states." Remarkably, when the naming process began, "Tipton" was considered, along with "Franklin" and "Tennessee."

Colonel John's wife Mary died giving birth to their ninth son, Jonathon Tipton, in 1776, the same year our nation was born. He is my great-great-great grandfather and was just getting his whiskers when the outlaw Franklander militia attacked his home. He grew up to carry on as a Tennessee senator, right where his daddy left off. His monument reads:

BORN AND REARED DURING TIMES THAT TRIED MEN'S SOULS

And to that I will answer, just as his father might have, "Hell Yeah!"

The author, Alice Tipton LaFleur, with her husband Rick and their French bulldog Ipsa, on the grounds of the Tipton-Haynes house, built 1784, Johnson City, Tennessee; photo: Matthew Frye, Tipton-Haynes State Historic Site

Chapter 3

RICH IN SOME WAYS, POOR IN OTHERS

As noted earlier, my grandfather, Dr. Paul Light Tipton, won the genetic bonanza for memory and came into the world equipped with total recall. He could actively remember and visualize anything that interested him, and this included large chunks of text and whole maps, so his mental feats weren't limited to things he directly experienced. He used this ability to great advantage as a physician and was acknowledged as an exacting diagnostician. He was his own medical database, never forgetting a symptom or its context.

Despite being an accomplished healer, Dr. Tipton's personality was off-putting and combative. His sense of humor was biting, using that sharp mind of his to humiliate and confuse people. In my experience, the only time his downturned mouth inverted to breach his cheeks was when he got the better of someone. If he got tickled, his face would turn pink, breaking into separate parts until he wheezed out silent laughter, his eyes getting all runny. It was unsettling, rare and to be avoided.

He was 73 when I was born, so I knew him only as an old man. Here are my impressions:

He'd always take dessert first, while we waited at the table for him to methodically finish his treat.

He'd plop his teeth in a glass of milk after meals, the fake gums sliding in and out of view if you watched.

He'd tape around his right index finger, covering an oozy wound from years of taking open X-rays.

He'd whittle pieces of wood, producing only sharpened ends in reflexive fidgeting to keep his hands busy.

He'd call black people "Negra," instead of the other "N" word, showing off that he wasn't a racist.

He'd enjoy arguing for its own sake, pointedly taking a contrarian side to grind any topic into dust.

He'd be dismissive of people after he baited them with his calculated opinions of contempt or praise.

Whenever I looked at my beautiful, sweet grandmother, Hettie Newfield Baird (Tipton), she seemed to be as flat as a swatted bug. I was mystified. Why him?

My father's mother, Miss Hettie, and her people hailed from the "Boot Heel Region" of southeast Missouri. Early in the 19th century the regional topography of this area was altered by a gigantic quake along the New Madrid seismic zone. The heaving caused the Mississippi River to flow backwards and set bells ringing as far away as Washington D.C. The big shake dumped tons of rich earthy mud onto what would someday become the vast stretches of farmland called "America's Breadbasket."

The geologic event is well described in a *Wikipedia* article ("1811–12 New Madrid earthquakes"):

> [It was] an intense intraplate earthquake series beginning with an initial pair of very large earthquakes on December 16, 1811. They remain the most powerful earthquakes to hit the contiguous United States east of the Rocky Mountains in recorded history.

Forty years after that quake, my grandmother's people arrived to settle in this thicket of rich bottomland with the idea of creating a working plantation. It was rough going in a thatchy swamp.

Two incidents, described by my great uncle, A. T. Douglass, in the following transcriptions from Missouri's Dunklin County Historical Society (Book 1, p. 488), clearly illustrate the challenges Miss Hettie's family met:

> There was a story about "dense woods" that has been handed down through the family. It is that once Grandpa and Grandma moved into a house that...was hard to find because it was surrounded by dense woods. One day the boys had gone away on an errand of some kind and on returning couldn't find the house. They felt they were near, so they called out until they were heard, and someone fired the gun so they would know which direction to take home.

Note the reference to "the" gun. They were so frugal it was probably the only one they had. After a decade of blisters forming over calluses trying to tame such a wilderness, my ancestors, Alexander Douglass and his wife Elizabeth Mott, along with their nine children, saw everything they had labored into existence on their meager farm burned to nothing during the Civil War. They had been rightly targeted as Rebels by Federal forces.

More from A. T. Douglass' account:

> How complete their destruction may be better realized by the scene that confronted Grandfather Douglass upon his return

to the plantation. Everything was in ruins and the smoke not cleared away; meat from the smokehouse was still sizzling and embers still smouldering (sic) where once his house had stood; nothing had been saved, and no place to rest his troubled head; even his neighbors were forbidden, under dire penalty, to give him aid; they could not even offer him shelter for the night.

In some ways the family had been spared. If Alexander Douglass had been at home, he would have been shot as "head of household," just as the Yankee soldiers had shot the wounded Confederate soldier they had been hiding in an outbuilding and their neighbor, "Doc" Baker, from across the way. The family rebuilt, but 15 years later, shortly after my great-great grandfather Alexander was lost to snakebite, it happened again.

Recently widowed, Elizabeth Mott Douglass and two of her children experienced yet another house on fire. Her other seven children were spared this traumatic déjà vu, all married and gone, but one son and their youngest child, my great grandmother Lucy, were still on the farm. Lucy was 18 years old and relived the horror she had suffered as a toddler when witnessing the fierce Union soldiers ransacking her home before torching it to cinders.

Two of the Douglass boys, J.M. and A.W., arranged to rebuild the family home for the second time, but decided to change the family's fortune by situating it away from the farm. They picked a piece of high ground that had been kicked up from the Missouri swampland during the 1811 tectonic shift. They tasked themselves with deconstructing an abandoned, but stately old residence from the nearby town of Kennett, and made sure each board of carefully numbered timber was put back in its right place on that pretty rise of land. The site had long been referred to as "Horse Island" by the locals, but the family decided to rename it "Senath" for A.W. Douglass' wife, since he and she had been instrumental in this last incarnation of the family home.

On June 16th, 1880, the same year her brothers finished the new place, Miss Lucy A. Douglass married James M. Baird. Young Lucy was introduced to her groom-to-be over at Cotton Plant, where her family purchased farm supplies. He was from nearby Arcadia and a recent hire at the dry-goods store, Langston & Sons. Since young Mr. Baird was staying with her sister and brother-in-law, Mr. Satterfield, Lucy had double pretense to speak to this tall handsome blue-eyed man.

Lucy Douglass Baird   *James M. Baird*

Lucy figured to consolidate her chores for more free time and on those days she could manage it, she'd saddle up and head on over to Cotton Plant. If James Baird wasn't at her sister's, she'd find reason to buy a little necessity from the store where he clerked. Eventually she managed to capture his exclusive attention and he married her. Within a decade they had three children, Margaret, who died at age seven, Huldah, who was born the same sad year they lost Margaret, and Hettie Newfield Baird, who arrived two years later in 1891.

The night my grandmother Hettie was born it was the autumnal equinox and 80 years since the New Madrid Fault had rearranged the earth beneath her. It was during a time of calm and it must have seemed a certainty to Mother Lucy that every light in the sky was lit for her. She had good reason to feel blessed. The land surrounding their house was known as "Senath," an up and coming town. While Lucy stayed home and reigned over a virtual community center, her enterprising husband (partnering with her brother J. M. Douglass) had developed J.M. Baird & Co., a mercantile business which brought in homesteaders looking for work and boasted the sole regional cotton gin.

The Baird house was known to welcome travelers in as guests. Mother Lucy offered snuff for the ladies and tobacco for the gents, "settin' them down" on her big wrap porch surrounded by flowers. She kept the raised planters her husband built filled year-round with color and fragrance. Company was always encouraged to linger.

Flowers were Lucy's hobby, but they were far more than that. She wanted to share her bounty. She had called on Jesus to face down a father-killing snake, two fires that had erased two homes and her firstborn's death. Sure that God's favor came at a price, she doubled down on proselytizing and prayer. It was penance in the form of the rich giving to the poor, but in her case it was the blessed saving the sinners, flowers and all.

Just by being part of the hometown founder's family, my grandmother, Miss Hettie Baird, was the sweetheart of Senath, Missouri. She was beautiful, graceful, spirited and driven. She distinguished herself by going to college to earn a degree in music and being the first female in town to wear split-skirts so she could sit horses astride instead of side-saddle. I have an old 78 rpm record with a song titled "Samson and Delilah" that she recorded for my father when he was serving in WW2. It's scratchy and barely audible, but her clear soprano is without a hint of tremolo. She was quietly proud of her voice.

*Postcard from Lyman to
Hettie Baird*

Mother Lucy kept close watch over her two surviving daughters, Huldah and Hettie, and since she was an ardent Southern Baptist, the girls were rarely allowed to sing outside of church. They couldn't go to dances either. I have a postcard sent to Miss Hettie from a young man named Lyman. Printed on the front is a picture of him standing next to a horse. The card has no date, but it is addressed to Hettie in Iowa, where she earned her music degree.

Her father's obituary, published in the *Dunklin Democrat,* March 4, 1910, states:

He acquired a nice lot of land, provided against financial misfortune with ample life insurance and left a nice property. Of the children born of his marriage, two survive, these being Mrs. Huldah Story, wife of the cashier of the Citizen Bank, of Senath, and Miss Hettie Baird. The latter was in Des Moines, Iowa, at school when her father died.

So the postcard to Iowa from Lyman was likely mailed sometime around her father's death, February 26, 1910.

The note written on the back of the card reads:

> Here is a picture of our trotting horse – has a record of 2/15, that is can trot a mile in 2 minutes + 15 seconds. The gentleman holding him can trot a mile in nothing. Come down to Sikeston [Missouri] & I will show you how bad we can beat an auto, L. A. M. [or possibly L. A. W. – Lyman's last initial is indecipherable due to the flourish he swirled around his signature.]

Hettie Newfield Baird, age 19

I haven't been able to identify the flamboyant young suitor, but it's interesting that my grandmother feels compelled to add this plea on the back:

> Here is a card I got from Lyman today. Don't destroy it.

That is a telling piece of evidence showing how closely monitored Miss Hettie was, even to the extent of having no privacy in her correspondence while away at college, where she lived under the close care of relatives.

I also have a picture of my grandmother dated 1910, the same year her father died and she was being courted by Lyman; she was 19. It's a full length profile showing the dress style of the time, but there is no smile under her large sunhat. My grandmother never smiled for pictures and I once thought it was a throwback from the old, rigid daguerreotype poses, but I now believe she considered smiling for the camera a sin of vanity. Both she and Huldah were instructed against sinful behaviors and told by their mother to pour the devil liquor down the drain if found in the house. They looked for it everywhere – their father, old man Baird, had issues of his own.

Chapter 4

DR. TIPTON AND MISS HETTIE

When my grandfather Paul Light Tipton married innocent Hettie Newfield Baird he was 11 years her senior, had balding red hair, a downturned mouth, acid blue eyes, large square shoulders and a deep barrel chest. By then her father had been dead four years, her sister had already married and her mother was consumed in every aspect of testimonial outreach. For generations Miss Hettie's people and Dr. Tipton's people had been frontiersmen heading down the same mountain passes, migrating south along the old buffalo trails Native Americans had been using for millennia, leading further out along the western slope of the Appalachians to arrive in this fertile bog flanking the time-worn Ozark Mountains. There my grandfather came to woo my lovely grandmother away from her family. Staunch Mother Lucy never saw him coming.

Paul L. Tipton was born in Dyersburg, not too far from Senath, on the other side of the Mississippi River in Tennessee. Two Tipton brothers had married two Light sisters and Paul was born to one of these pairs. He was the only male of six children and spoiled by his five doting sisters, even more so after their mother, Sallie Light (Tipton), died when he was a teenager.

Paul's aunt, Molly Light (Tipton), had two children, a girl and a boy, and had been widowed for some years when her sister Sally died. His father, Molly, and the eight first cousins then all lived together in the old "Light House" in Dyer County as a blended family. Paul and cousin Mary, his "double first," were near in age and the two

Paul Light Tipton, with his five sisters

The Light estate, Dyersburg, Tennessee

became lifelong friends. As an adult, he would visit her family in Tennessee and go fox hunting with her husband and son. The son, Dr. Joe Moody, is now in his 90s, and he shared his recollection of my grandfather's purebred Walker Foxhounds when I contacted him for Tipton family memories. Our exchanges forced up a mental snapshot of an incident I had long forgotten.

Grandfather Tipton must have been around 83; I was almost six, wearing a yellow sweater. My parents had stopped for a visit before taking us overseas. I remember a pack of sleeping hounds huddled in the back of a beige "woody" station wagon. In my mind everything is a dull brown; my grandfather's old khaki shirt and pants, the dusty wooden house and the big liver-spotted dogs. Over to the side was their fenced in area of scuffed up dirt, but on that day my grandfather had decided to let the pack run loose, to chase a scent, as he settled himself on the porch to whittle.

It didn't seem like my grandfather was doing much, but I got quickly shushed so he could concentrate. In the distance the hounds gave voice. The changing register of their baying let him know whether they had found or lost the trail, flushed their quarry, or were in the process of boxing that critter in. Studying his face as he peered into the sound, it looked as though he was watching the dogs work. I was made to understand they were under his command and trained not to kill, acting only as his sentinels. But when they made that high tight yodeling noise, he could either keep them on task or release them by blowing into the bull's horn he kept hanging nearby on a leather strap.

The scene is so vivid, it must have been the same day I tripped and sliced the artery on the underside of my right wrist. The bright red quickly soaking into the yellow ridges and traveling up the cuff of my cotton sweater presents itself clearly in my mind. I was where I wasn't supposed to be, down on all fours, inside the double-fenced edge of the dog pen. I could smell the sticky tan cornmeal hash in their feed bowls as I looked down at my wrist. I remember it being close between the fences, a cramped space littered with leaves, trash and broken glass that only I could fit into. I have no sense of my grandfather stitching in the sutures, but I can still see the thick scar they left behind.

In an excerpt from his "Autobiographical Sketch of Dr. Paul L. Tipton," my grandfather wrote this about himself:

> He graduated from the University of Tennessee Medical School and took up residency in surgery at Tulane University in New Orleans. Rather than practicing his specialty in a large city where facilities were available, he preferred a smaller community where the services of a family physician were so desperately needed, and he practiced in Senath, Caruthersville and Blytheville, and became Chief of Staff at the Blytheville Hospital.

My grandfather had more than just a capacious memory for detail, he was also fully ambidextrous. He could sign his name with either hand and never had to move around the operating table while performing surgery. This is no trivial gift. Until he developed tremors from holding patients under the early X-ray cones, he literally had two hands he could control with equal precision. As a hobby he made fishing rods, twining a series of colored threads down a pole to anchor graduated loops. He would also attach skittery feathers onto barbed hooks for snatching bluegill and bass out of the water. As a child I thought they were pretty, the work being so tight and precise it was hard finding the knots.

It's intriguing to me that my grandfather went back home after being exposed to the vibrant city of New Orleans, but he chose Senath, not 50 miles away from where he grew up. That he went where he could do the most good is certainly true, but it wouldn't have taken

Tacky party, Paul Tipton in hat, fourth from left

long for Dr. Tipton to spy the pretty Miss Hettie Baird, if he wasn't already in full pursuit. After all, he was an exacting man making his plans. I have a picture of him in 1911, three years before they were married, at what was colloquially termed a "tacky party." These were exclusive gatherings where young men would get together to act the fool, grandstand for each other and wear silly hats. Maybe they'd drink a little whiskey and swear for each other, but it was mainly a safe place where men could act out, circumventing the women folk. The photograph was taken in Senath, Missouri.

I speculate that Miss Hettie would have been aware of Dr. Tipton too, as he was of her. Hers was a very small pond with a population of 1,000 souls at most. A new physician in town would be big news. He also had a certain presence; he was a certain kind of man. Cut from the same bolt of cloth that had produced the starchy Colonel John Tipton, he trusted his instincts, was convinced of his own worth and, because of his unusual upbringing, was completely at ease around women. He was a "catch" by any measure, but if my grandmother ever wondered if she had somehow lured him into marriage, she was being naïve. Bait, by definition, is already in a trap.

Hettie Baird Tipton

Paul Light Tipton

Chapter 5

THE TIPTON HOUSEHOLD

In order to respond to the intense interest shown by Dr. Tipton, Miss Hettie had broken off her long engagement to Lyman. She tactfully sent his ring back in a box containing another item, so when he opened the package he wouldn't be shamed in front of his family. He could show them the benign memento instead. She knew he would be heartbroken by her decision and didn't want to cause him more pain.

On April 15, 1914, Dr. Paul Light Tipton and Miss Hettie Newfield Baird were married, and my father, James Baird Tipton, was born just ten months later, on Groundhog's Day. After the birth many people were counting backwards on their fingers, just to make sure. Richard Pike Tipton followed two years later and the Paul Light Tipton family was complete. Two boys were just what Dr. Tipton wanted and my grandmother never bore another child. I know she had "female problems," and I know he performed her hysterectomy. What I don't know is when that happened, just that it did.

Grandmother Lucy Baird with baby Jim Tipton

My grandmother had left a family with no father and no brothers to become the centerpiece of three men. Each of them, in his own way, competed for her attention. She was their queen. Dr. Tipton was a devout outdoorsman — reminiscent of his distant ancestor Tibba — and he taught his boys to hunt, fish, camp and track early in their young lives. He would test their mettle by taking the whole family deep into the Ozarks for a week or more, going with nothing but guns, poles and a few rudimentary provisions. On these trips they'd head so far into the wild they rarely spotted smoke from another campfire.

The men would bring their kill to Mother Hettie as offerings, to skin and dress. They listened whenever she broke into singing old-timey hymns and stayed available to help with the meals she created for them, often finding wild mushrooms and greens she could use nearby. She soon became reputed as a fabulous game cook and it was rustic high fun as the boys developed survival skills and grew confident in their bodies. Miss Hettie told me my father could drink over a gallon of milk a day, once growing more than seven inches in a single year. I have a picture of him where his legs look too long for the skinny little boy on top, but that awkward stage didn't last. His physique took after the Baird side of the family and he topped out somewhere over 6'2", with the beautiful posture of his

Jim and his younger brother, Richard (known to many as "Tip" or "Dick")

mother and a long easy gait.

The early years of my grandparents' marriage were probably my grandmother's best, but my grandfather eventually showed his true nature. Her gentle temperament was no match for such a bull-headed man. The Douglass farm, owned in equal shares by the three remaining Bairds — Mother Lucy, Huldah and Miss Hettie — was sold to bolster the faltering J. M. & Baird store finances. The Great Depression was looming and selling the homestead during the growing recession may have been a wise move before prices plummeted, but it was a

Jim Tipton as a long-legged youngster

decision Dr. Tipton vehemently opposed. He believed owning land was the only sure bet and the best way to fend off disaster.

Feeling his determination and intellect overruled, he decided it was Huldah's husband, the banker, who was behind the land's sale and forbade my grandmother from ever seeing her sister or her sister's family again. In a further act of retribution Dr. Tipton took his grievance against his brother-in-law into their Masonic Temple, lobbying unsuccessfully to revoke his membership and accusing him of forging my grandmother's signature to get at the farm's deed.

The Baird homestead and farm workers, on the outskirts of Senath, Missouri

I had always heard that Miss Hettie first found out about the sale of the family farm when she saw it posted in the morning paper. Legally, if the three-way ownership could go forward on closing with a simple majority of only two signatures, her brother-in-law, O.H. Story, may have been unjustly slandered by my grandfather. Hettie wouldn't have had to sign anything for the sale to be legal. It has proved impossible for me to discover the particulars, but regardless, speaking against a fraternal brother is never tolerated and in 1918 my grandfather's name dropped off the Senath Masonic Lodge roster.

Dr. Tipton wrote the following in the same autobiographical sketch cited above, a document originally composed by him for his own obituary:

He attained the 32nd degree in the Masons, a Knight Templar.

He went on to join another lodge, but he never talked to his brother-in-law again. He never mended the rift. He may have been too proud, but Miss Hettie was proud too. Being so high and falling so low in a town so small must have been beyond galling. The loose talk was bad enough, but people feeling sorry for her would rankle like nothing else could have. Surrounded, she pulled in harder. She held her head higher and spoke her words softer. She carried on.

Over the years I know my grandmother sometimes spent time with her sister, but it was always on the sly. When Mother Lucy was too old to care for her flower beds, she moved in with her daughter, Huldah Story, until her death in 1943. Perhaps this provided a pathway for the sisters to meet, but it was never acknowledged by Dr. Tipton. He could never give her a reprieve on that front. He was unbending.

The family left Senath around 1924 for Caruthersville, Missouri, a larger town, where they stayed for about three years. Dr. Tipton was still in general practice, but that all changed when he next moved his family to Blytheville, Arkansas, about 25 miles west of Senath, and acquired his own hospital. These may qualify as my grandfather's best years. I have a 1929 group photo of Dr. Tipton and his partner Dr. Morris standing behind a group of 10 nursing graduates on the steps of the Blytheville Teaching Hospital. Between the two physicians stands Miss Hettie, as testament to her essential role in the success of her husband's business venture.

She was responsible for laundry, cleaning, meals and everything else a patient might remember in terms of their non-medical experience. At the time, flowers were thought to be harmful because they sucked oxygen out of the air. Each evening she patrolled the sickroom ward, looking in on her charges. She dutifully took all flowers out into the hall for the patients' protection and returned them the next morning to brighten their day.

My grandmother never lived in Senath again, but they didn't stay situated in Blytheville forever either. By the mid-1940s Dr. Tipton was seriously ill and wasting away with thyrotoxicosis, so he delivered himself to the famous Cleveland Clinic for help. Uncharacteristically out of his depth, he had reached out. He must have been terrified. It was determined that his heart was too weak to survive an operation, so he was "sent home to die." He sold the clinic and bought a square mile of Missouri farmland with the proceeds. After they put their belongings into storage, Miss Hettie and Dr. Tipton started on a journey to say goodbye to all his favorite haunts.

They stayed in a cabin cantilevered over the Eleven Point River in Riverton, Missouri, and rented a fish-camp by the ocean in Gulf Shores,

Alabama, where they also took a place on Lake Martin in Elmore County. They visited family in Texas, California and Tennessee. They basically continued to live in nomadic transit, going back again and again to these same places, until moving in with my parents and me in 1968. Their sojourn lasted 20 years, and though my grandfather's thyroid malady had long since "burned itself out," leaving him alive and whole, my grandmother had burned out too. She made her domestic space wherever they landed, all of her possessions stored away, traveling with a man who lived in his head and always arriving as a guest.

Dr. Paul Light Tipton during his illness, July 11, 1943

Dr. Paul L. Tipton died in 1971; he was 92. At the time, Miss Hettie was still lithe and elegant at 81 and was often mistaken for my father's wife instead of his mother. Eventually she developed a similar confusion and, instead of "Jimmie," started calling him "Dad," her pet name for Dr. Tipton. Soon she began referring to my mother as "that woman" while pulling on my father to come to bed with her. It irked him to no end, but my grandfather must have been something to miss, since she was still so interested. She drove my mother crazy too. She kept killing the houseplants by sneaking them outside at night, so they wouldn't asphyxiate us all.

When my grandmother's slow dementia eventually threatened her safety, she was put in a "rest home." At first she clamped her teeth shut and refused to eat food, but they took her dentures away so they could force feed her. She lived to be 98 years old, her last years curled into a fetal position. Her roommate was a stroke victim who could only scream, "A, B, C, D...GODDAMN SON-OF-A-BITCH," over and over, all day long. It was more than Miss Hettie could say.

Blytheville Hospital. Dr. Paul Tipton and Hettie Tipton,
upper left, with Dr. Morris and 10 nurse graduates,
1929

Chapter 6

LIFE CAN BE A GAME

Writing about my father's youth is much harder for me than writing about my mother's. It's like looking through binoculars from the wrong end; everything's there, but it's obscure and distant. If my father's people are any measure, Missouri's motto as the "show me" state was picked for good reason. My father wasn't much of a talker and my grandparents weren't either. Stoic, insular and mutually supportive, they were a monolithic blind spot to me. When I was in high school, the three of them would often compare how little sleep they needed, but never told what compelled them to get out of bed in the first place.

My father Jim and his brother Tip sought the pride of their father and admired both his awesome intellect and his physicality. He was a stern patriarch and committed to excellence. He forcefully showed disapproval when either of his sons missed his bar of high expectations, but still maintained a curiosity about the whys of their motivation. He would drill them, forcing them to fend off his criticism with rational explanation. This disciplinary tactic forced them to become circumspect in their judgement, knowing they would have to own their choices. Dr. Tipton was formidable and his boys always had to square with him. He was a bear of a man.

When the Tipton family moved to Blytheville, Arkansas, life became more complicated for my father. The town's population was five times larger than Caruthersville's and ten times larger than Senath's. Dr. Tipton was busy with his hospital, a place where he could practice surgery in earnest, and Miss Hettie, always a capable woman, was preoccupied with being the administrator for his nursing staff. The boys were required to negotiate Blytheville's much bigger school without complaint.

In 1982 my father responded to a request from a colleague to share his memories of leading the 363rd fighter group in WW2 and his personal philosophy of command. The document he produced is 85 numbered pages of hurried remarks, extemporaneously handwritten in pencil on lined paper. It has strike-outs, erasures and notes with arrows pointing to previous remarks. Obviously my mother was supposed to edit and type it up for him, but I doubt it ever got revised or mailed to anyone. The content was too personal and in the last few pages he laments the unsuitability of what he had written. Without meaning to, my father had composed a memoir. The opening of this informal chronicle of his life illustrates Jim Tipton's defining humility:

> In the first place I dislike to talk about me; it makes me uncomfortable. When I am the subject, even indirectly, the pain (of writing) is multiplied several fold.

The move to Arkansas had come when Jim was entering high school and just as he hit his first growth spurt. He was shy and quiet, didn't mind being left alone and regularly pestered the librarian in his new hometown for more of the "pulp hero" type books he devoured like candy. He read about Genghis Khan, King Arthur and Lawrence of Arabia. He liked the authors Kipling, Doyle and Poe. He read adventure, science fiction and detective novels. But literature about the solo trans-Atlantic flights of Charles Lindbergh and the heroic acts of the WW1 doughboys found him where he lived. He determined that being an aviator was the one thing he wanted out of life, and not just any aviator, but an Ace, and he worried whether there might not be any frontiers left to conquer or wars left to fight when he got old enough to fly.

Jim Tipton wrote this of himself in his 1982 memoir:

> During my second year in high school the student body elected me "most conceited." I was astounded. I had no close friends, had become a bookworm and was so timid that I blushed if anyone spoke to me. Over the years I ceased to blush, but I haven't changed much. My introversion frequently strikes others as self-satisfaction. Simultaneously, my passionate practice of modesty, the old strong-but-silent syndrome, became a defense mechanism as well as a tenet and it too often was interpreted as ostentation or complacency. If my personality rasped people for wrong reasons, so be it. Since popularity, politics, and dictatorship objectives held no attractions for me, my alter-ego didn't bother me too much.

Dr. Tipton wrote this of himself in third person for his own obituary:

> He was an ardent fan of athletic groups, and offered his services freely to all the young people participating in football, basketball, track, etc.

That testimonial may have been true, but Dr. Tipton was completely opposed to his own boys playing football. In his practice, my grandfather had seen injuries from concussions and was certain they cost the young men their brain power. Many of his odd ideas (sweets before a meal are healthier, too much sun is bad, spicy foods inhibit stomach disease and smoke causes cancer) were forward-thinking for the times; he was right about those as yet unproven edicts and right about the dangers of football as well. But his older son defied him. I'm not sure which year young Jim started playing the game, but I know he had to go up against Dr. Tipton to do it.

TIPTONS OF TECH AND BLYTHEVILLE A

✧ ✧ ✧   ✧ ✧ ✧   ✧ ✧ ✧

Jimmy of Chickasaws And Harry of Jackets Will Forget Relationship When Te

BY WILSON MURRAH.

Tipton vs. Tipton, will be the feature of the annual battle between the Tech High Yellowjackets and the Blytheville Chickasaws tomorrow night on Haley Field. Jimmy Tipton is captain and center of Blytheville and Harry Tipton is halfback for the Yellowjackets.

The two Tiptons will discard their blood kin, cousins, and give their best to the fight on the chalkboard. Jimmy Tipton is being hailed as the best center developed on the Blytheville squad since the days when Jess Eberdt paraded the pivot position in

tribe of the Chickasaws. Jimmy weighs around 175 pounds and his spectacular tackling has marked him as a formidable contender for all-state honors.

Harry Tipton tips the beam at weight handicap with his fighting around 150 pounds but offsets the aggressiveness. Coach Charley Jamerson had the following to

Oppose Tech Friday Night

CAPT. JIMMY TIPTON, C.,
Blytheville High.

TOM SHORT, H.B.,
Blytheville High.

Tipton vs. Tipton, Blytheville, Arkansas, newspaper clipping

My father never got dementia from playing sports, but he often complained about his poor memory. As a child I was warned to never touch his nose because he didn't like it. Football helmets in the 1930s were made of thick hard leather, without faceguards, and his nose had been broken several times. Once, taking a taxi home after an operation, he was in so much pain that he had the driver stop so he could get out, bend over the shoulder of the road and yank the wads of bloody gauze out of his face. Like an animal, he was trying to relieve the pressure, but his nose never looked the same again.

During his senior year in high school, my father applied to the U.S. Military Academy in West Point, New York, and the Naval Academy in Annapolis, Maryland – anything that would get him in a plane – but it was all to no effect, as there were few appointments that year. He was graduating in 1932, the middle of the Great Depression, and it was hard going all around. Jobs were scarce and those who could afford it went to college, and most who did ended up taking teaching positions instead of working in their field. Jim knew he'd hate being stuck inside a school, at a desk, grounded. He formulated another way in; he would find a way to join the elite Flying Cadets – think the 1930s radio serial, "The Air Adventures of Jimmie Allen." All he had to do was get somebody's attention.

Despite the doctor's concern for his son, Jim had performed well enough in high school football to be offered scholarships from colleges all over the country. He and his father had finally come to terms. Dr. Tipton had to admit that his son's decision to join the football team had paid off, especially with the economy as it was. He even attended a few games after Jim was made team captain, though it was hard to watch the rough contact. It was understood by Dr. Tipton that his boy was born to compete, lettering in basketball, track and javelin throw, while staying fit off-season by playing county league baseball, when he wasn't too busy working as a lifeguard. There was no holding him down.

Jim eventually accepted a football scholarship to attend the University of Alabama, since it offered an Aeronautical Engineering degree and advanced ROTC, all of which fit into his master plan of getting into the United States Army Air Corps. And he added a new goal: not only did he want to be an Ace, he wanted to make the All-American team at his new school in Tuscaloosa.

Leaving home was hard for him and in many ways he wished he could stay. He loved his family, especially his mother. She often sang for his high school's student assembly and he wasn't at all embarrassed to be demonstrative in his pride for her, despite the wisecracks coming from his small group of friends. He was okay with being called a "mama's boy" and, heckling aside, he would miss seeing her excitement before singing solo for an audience other than their church.

Chapter 7

THE LITTLE HOUSEHOLD

Unlike Jim Tipton, Ann Little did not have warm feelings about her mother. I feel sure it was to my grandmother's uncomfortable dismay to find herself with child in her 40th year. The idea of another baby would have been daunting to my grandfather as well, since he was closing in on 50 when Ann arrived in the fall of 1914. My mother often insisted that her parents' marriage was a distant one and her birth only a fluke. Blame it on those pesky hormonal spikes that lead to many a late-in-life indulgence, but surely Ann's creation was the quintessential menopause surprise, as well as my grandmother's only difficult birth.

My maternal grandmother, Mary Bellows Dodds (Mama Lit), was artistic, religious, opinionated and looked the epitome of an 1800s "Gibson Girl" in the ¾ length, larger-than-life portrait which my Aunt Sue eventually had cut down to fit a more manageable, waist-up sized frame. From it she gazes out past you with a relaxed hand holding a string of pearls pulled across the neckline of a gauzy, off-the-shoulder evening dress. The pose is classic Victorian, and she is softly pretty with her hair piled up in that glorious bouffant style of the late 1800s.

Mary Bellows Dodds Little   *Seelye William Little*

Mama Lit was a woman in motion and considered herself to be a working artist. She would often escape her domestic sphere in Rochester, New York, and join her brother in New York City, where they shared a studio. My Great Uncle Arthur C. Dodds was Mama Lit's business partner as well as being family and her close friend. He was once described to me as the first ever to use the term "interior decorator" in explaining what he did to earn his keep. My mother thought he had actually invented the term, and I imagine the siblings had wonderful times working together as a part of the burgeoning artist community in America's paragon of urban life. Mama Lit was more of a break-even kind of artist than truly self-supporting, but she and her brother worked well together, and he valued her strong opinions, her artistic eye and her relentless energy.

In contrast, I believe my Great Uncle Arthur was a proven New York success, but the only snippets of trivia I know about his sense of style had to do with his own home (which he termed "the Dodd-damned mill"), where he added a non-functional staircase to the corner of a large dreary room to give it "warmth" and kept the dead, dried-up hedge surrounding his house painted a bright green, apparently because he liked the gnarly shapes of its leafless branches. When questioned about these odd choices, he would point out the obvious. The attractive shrubbery was maintenance free and the outrageous staircase a provocative conversation piece.

I have a picture of Mama Lit standing with Uncle Arthur seated beside her. It shows him to be a trim and handsome

Mama Lit and her brother Uncle Arthur

dresser. He was also a determined bachelor and a discreetly un-closeted, widely known homosexual. He died in 1934 after he fell from a tree when he was in his 60s. My grandmother successfully sued his insurance company in the New York State Supreme Court by proving that "Falling from a balcony while pruning a tree is not a pre-existing condition." The woman was no slouch, but then, neither was he.

The year Mama Lit passed away was 1948, five years before my birth. She announced she was tired, drove herself home, went to bed, fell asleep and died. In some ways she approached death in the same straightforward way she lived. My mother never explained why the two of them had strained relations, but there were hints. She would often reference the fact that Mama Lit would advise other people on how to do things she didn't do herself. Mother would tell this in an amusing way, but my grandmother apparently made arch observations on many topics and "had something to say about everything." My mother found this off-putting.

Mama Lit was also a great kidder, always keeping the center of attention for herself. She was adept at using black humor for its shock value, often introducing six-year-old Ann Little as her "posthumous child." The self-depreciative quip was funny, but to young Ann the laughter seemed pointed directly at her, insulting and embarrassing for reasons she couldn't quite grasp.

Then there was her sister Jane. Though she never directly said it, I think my mother felt less loved by Mama Lit in comparison to Jane. To be fair, Mama Lit also got laughs when she referred to her older daughter as "my dark child," due to Jane's swarthy coloring, body hair, and the barely noticeable down on her upper lip. But Jane wasn't offended by the joke at her expense. She knew how attractive she was even if she did have a slight moustache. She was also the perfect counterpart for their mother, who was renowned for her tireless pursuit of high art. Jane was gifted in that direction.

From her perspective, my grandmother already had her completed family with Uncle Bill, Uncle Jim and then Aunt Jane, born like links in a chain in 1906, '07 and '10 respectively. The physical complications leading up to Ann's much later birth and the arduous delivery may have compromised the initial bonds between mother and child. Or, just as easily, they might have found themselves increasingly distant as time went on, having less and less in common.

Jane, Bill, Ann (age one), and Jim with Mama Lit

Regardless, Ann clearly adored her sister Jane and understood why their mother so loved her. Everyone did. She was vivacious, relaxed and a delightful wit in her own right. In her teens, Jane and her close friend Betty Farley would frequent New York City just to visit Uncle Arthur and relish the "Big Apple" experience. He loved fashion and knew all the best shops in town. He had an inside track with merchants in the clothing district and escorted the girls around to haggle good deals for them.

Once, Aunt Jane "shocked the whole town of Rochester" when she came home from one of those uptown sprees sporting a shingle haircut. The modern, boyish look complemented her dark straight hair, and the bangs formed a frame around her black-brown eyes. Always ahead of the trends, Jane wore pug shoes, rolled stockings, dresses belted low-hip, and topped it all off with long "shrugs" of beads draping down from around her neck. In those days it was her rule never to leave home without her unbuckled galoshes causing a rhythmic flapping sound with every step. She was a bona fide "flapper."

During the Roaring Twenties and Prohibition, young Ann longed to be just like her big sister. She wanted to sneak out, dance till late-night and smoke cigarettes in speakeasies where bands played till dawn. She wanted to wear short dresses, sleek her hair into a bob and drink bootleg whiskey served from bathtubs. Ann was desperate to be part of the wild New York scene, but she was too young. She contented herself with keeping her big sister's secret life away from their snoopy mother by supporting Jane's improvised white lies. Mama Lit would hardly have approved of the nighttime doings of the "Jazz Age."

If Ann's mother-daughter interactions weren't very satisfactory, I believe the opposite was true of her dealings with her father, Dr. Seelye William Little, commonly known as Dr. Lit. She was his youngest child and therefore considered herself to be his favorite, although all of his children felt the same way. He was that kind of a man.

Early in my grandparents' romance there were almost daily letters exchanged between young Mary Dodds (she was 9 years his junior) and my grandfather, Seelye Little. Mama Lit saved all of them in a shoe box. The affair was still new and he was trying to coax her to come back from her life in New York City to be his wife. He would often work as a

Dr. Seelye William Little courting Mary Bellows Dodds

handyman at the old Dodds place, called the Chamberlin House, with the intention of ingratiating himself with her parents as a potential son-in-law. He was quite imaginative in his correspondence. In one letter he wrote of the "forlorn cerise" paint color he had applied to her parents' walls and the flecks of "aching ochre" he routinely scrubbed from its cruddy front steps. Even chores were used to express his deep sentiment for her.

The marvelous shoebox I inherited with the hundreds of letters full of yearning and frustration addressed to "Little Sweets" and closing with "Au Revoir" span the decades from 1900 to the mid-1930s. They read like a time-capsule thread of narratives from Dr. Lit's point of view, running from my grandparents' dating phase all the way through to the end of their 36-year marriage.

Mary Dodds did not settle down or give up her art after she became Mrs. Little, so during the first decade of their marriage, whenever she left to design monograms or fabricate elaborate lampshades in the "Big City" for Uncle Arthur, Dr. Lit remained behind with the children. In his letters he sometimes questions her lack of business savvy as well as reminding her that the children need her and ask for their "mommy" at bedtime.

Meanwhile he was stretched thin between practicing medicine under his father, being tapped by his in-laws for sundry maintenance issues and dealing with the three children. By the end of this time period the "Little Sweets" salutation eventually gives way to a simple "Mary," but the letters were still posted almost daily and always filled with a unique wordplay.

I have two pieces of Mama Lit's art. One is a handmade christening gown that my mother, her sister, my sister, I and my daughter all wore. It hangs in a shadow box in my dining room. The other is a one inch, circular, filigree pendant I wear almost always. Both display Mama Lit's fierce dedication to her art. First, the delicate gown shows her skill at detail. The tiny tucks and layered embroidery are precise and fine, but my pendant reveals her determination.

Gold pendant with 31 diamonds, crafted by Mama Lit

It was originally crafted as a monogram-brooch to celebrate Ann Livingston Little's birth, and Mama Lit designed it to use up all of the 31 pieces of diamonds she had on hand. They are simple European or mine cuts of various sizes, with the exception of a larger pair of quarter carat, rose-cut diamonds – one each for the letters A and L (she didn't use my mother's middle initial, L, in the monogram, since Mama Lit wasn't keen on her mother-in-law, a Livingston).

She wanted to set the diamonds in the deep yellow of a 20-dollar U.S. coin, but when she took the gold piece to her jeweler, he resisted. It was "legal tender." It was "government property." It was a "criminal act!" Undeterred, Mama Lit next took the coin to her dentist, who had no qualms about melting money. He heated it up in a crucible, as if for a filling, and handed her back a warm lump of 22-karat gold, which she then presented to her jeweler. The inscription on the back reads, "A. Little" and "Rochester," as if any damn fool would know exactly who she was, or where that was, anywhere in the world.

Chapter 8

THE LITTLE RESIDENCES

Before Ann was born, the Little family had built a modest summer home near Rochester on Lake Ontario. They named it "Alouette" (French for a little bird, specifically a lark), and it was situated just east of Irondequoit Bay, near a stretch of untouched land called Big Woods. During construction, Mama Lit remarked, "Looks like a baked potato on a hill," but then Dr. Lit pointed out, "You can see the lake from every window," adding "though you may have to lean out very, very far, Little Sweets."

My grandfather wrote poems about Alouette. As two examples of his writing, I include a scan of his typescript of one of them, and here is another:

Home

Do you know why it seems to me
There's nothing left but memory
Of passing years. When Summer's gone?

And why I wait impatiently
For Summer of the year-to-be
When this year's summer's gone?

All other days in town I dwell;
But Summer days; then all is well –
I live at Alouette.

The family would stay on the bluff overlooking the water to escape the heat and dusty town clamor from late spring till early fall, and Dr. Lit would periodically leave them, going back to Rochester to attend to his duties via horse-drawn wagon. The troublesome mare reluctantly pulling him was "Mrs. Eddy," so named after Mary Baker Eddy, founder of the faith-healing cult known as Christian Scientists. It was all the rage among certain groups around town. The doctor would get sidelong looks from the newly recruited, who'd stopped using his services, as he urged his old nag forward with loud cursing, "Get on, Mrs. Eddy! Get on now!" It amused him to publicly scold the balking horse as he made his rounds.

Naturally Dr. Lit delivered all his own children at home, so when Ann's older sister Jane was born in August, she arrived in their

Alouette when it was first built

summer house, Alouette. The farmwomen in the area marveled at the easy birth and gossiped that Dr. Little was a "city" doctor and so deft a practitioner he could lift an infant by its feet and, just as the baby opened its mouth wide to yowl, pluck its tonsils out in so smooth a motion that the babe would hardly know what had happened. No muss, no fuss, and no scary medical procedure involving the dreaded ether gas.

Accurate or not, the doctor was known for his proficient work and droll turn of phrase. He was approachable to all manner of people and disbursed wisdom and expertise to family, friends, constituents and the broader medical community in letters, poems,

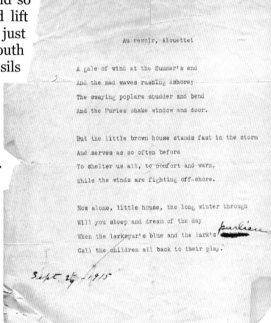

Poem typed by Dr. Little

Alouette, on a postcard from Dr. Lit to his sister Alice ("Topsy")

*Reverse of the postcard to Topsy, where Dr. Lit mentions his son Jim's
rock collection*

*Another bit of family lore about young Jim and the floor of his room had to
do with his allowance. He'd exchange it for pennies, close his eyes and spin
around, letting his handful of coins fly in all directions. Whenever he needed
cash, he would hunt around in his room for the loose change! This unusual
habit of squirreling away funds in odd places continued into Jim's adulthood.
He had little caches of subway tokens scattered all over New York. He hid
them in an "I spy with my little eye" kind of a way wherever he was and stayed
on the lookout for them, even years afterwards, whenever he took the subway.*

drawings and published medical treatises. He was both literate and whimsical, encouraging a gentle timbre to my mother's childhood.

Dr. Lit was an old-fashioned healer who worked out of his clinic on the first floor of their home, the corner of Plymouth Avenue and Troup Street. He had acquired the old Chamberlin House from his in-laws in 1913, just before Ann was born. It was situated a short distance down the street from his birthplace, 162 Plymouth Avenue, where he had lived comfortably with his bride Mary Dodds while apprenticing under his father, until his family grew too large with the unexpected arrival of child number four. He knew what he was getting into since he was intimate with the cantankerous old structure, but he needed the room, the price was right, and by then he was technically ready to have his own practice.

Playing an important role in my mother's life, the edifice at 107 Plymouth Avenue was originally built in the early 1840s as a residence for Captain James R. Chamberlin, a successful rubber merchant, Civil War veteran, and my great great grandfather on the Dodds side. It was so large it was eventually leased to different groups, including the Atkinson Female Seminary, a "school for young ladies." It was later razed by fire and though I never uncovered the cause, I did find the original 8x10, black and white photograph taken for the newspaper that shows the flames blazing out from the attic dormers. The date of the paper was clipped off, but it looks to be the late 1940s.

The old house was where my mother was born and where my grandfather saw his patients, unless he was out on house-calls or off dealing

The house at Plymouth and Troup on fire. Flames pour from the attic, where the Little women stayed during the Great Depression.

with an emergency in town. He had status and respectability, but the Littles would never be a wealthy family. In those days physicians received relatively poor amounts of cash for their services compared to what our modern medical doctors garner today, and he was often paid "in kind" with eggs or yard work or any other barter he could negotiate. This is how it was done — long hours, hard work, and little money. Being a doctor required a calling, like being a priest, a teacher or a soldier, and the good ones never said "no" to those with an affliction, even if the afflicted had nothing to offer in return.

Since Dr. Lit was rarely able to leave his practice, or the ever-present home repairs, and Mama Lit was often away pursuing her own interests, my mother had more paternal than maternal influence in her younger years than was typical for that era. Her father required Ann to learn self-reliance and allowed her to roam freely along Plymouth Avenue, between home and her grandparents' house, a well-defined block where she could walk to her school, the Livingston Park Seminary, and where she was permitted to play with the "proper" children of their neighborhood.

When Ann was growing up, the area was undergoing a transitional phase. The Third Ward, once referred to as "The Old Ruffled Shirt Ward," still housed some of the more eminent families, but they were leaving. As folks could afford more modern accommodations, they moved eastward and newcomers had slowly filtered in. Ann was strictly forbidden to visit anyone without a formal introduction, but she was a very social child. One day Dr. Lit witnessed her going into a stranger's house. She lied to him and explained it away when he confronted her with what he had seen. He let her lie and acted as though he believed her story, which made her guilt far worse. The uncomfortable feeling it gave her was still fresh in her mind, decades later, when she wrote in her memoir about abusing his trust that day.

At an appropriate age, Dr. Lit wisely presented Ann with a compact dark brown dog. It was at a perfect time in her young life for such responsibility and she promptly dubbed him Toqué, French for a kind of sable fur hat. The word also meant touched-in-the-head, zany, daffy or silly. Ann was given complete responsibility for Toqué, which included teaching him commands. One of his best tricks was balancing a treat on his nose until given the go-ahead to pop it airborne and gulp it down. Another favorite antic was self-taught. Whenever it occurred to him, or he met someone new, he would intentionally curl

Dr. Lit with Toqué

his upper lip. He seemed to enjoy making people laugh with his doggy smile. He was a well-known clown around their side of town.

There is an image of pre-adolescent Ann showing a dark haired, fit little girl with heavy-lidded hazel eyes and a sweet smile. She is kneeling with her arms around Toqué, and I recognize him as a bull. This breed of dog is noted for intelligence, strength and loyalty. My mother would later ascribe many of her most important lessons about the nature of obedience, trust and determination as coming from this early relationship. Toqué ran unleashed, but would always stop and return to her side when she whistled their special code, regardless of his important doggy business elsewhere.

Ann Little with Toqué

Chapter 9

THE GEOGRAPHY OF FORTUNE

My maternal grandfather was the fourth and last in a near uninterrupted, hundred year run of Dr. Littles in upstate New York. The "original" was Dr. David Little, and he lived from 1768 to 1832 in a settlement called Springfield just outside of Cherry Valley. His incredible story was so powerful and macabre that it was published over a century later in *The New Yorker* magazine.

The tale begins when he was asked to treat the aristocratic daughter of a close personal friend. The men's relationship quickly came undone when Dr. Little declared the man's daughter wasn't ailing, just pregnant. The resulting scandal, based on her unmarried "condition," turned even more tragic when she never gave birth while in confinement. The outraged father, feeling betrayed by his friend's incompetence, turned into a vindictive enemy and wrecked Dr. Little's professional reputation – even as his daughter carried a very rare, fossilized, lithopedion fetus in her womb.

The lithopedion fetus

Two years later the young woman died from a fever that was sweeping through their county. Within days of the burial, Dr. David Little used his dutiful freedman to hold a lantern above him as he unlawfully excavated the remains, after midnight, from her freshly dug grave in the family's plot. He was still convinced of his diagnosis and needed the truth. The assistant, now accomplice, was given enough hush-money for him to leave town and never be seen again.

I can't imagine the nerve it took for those two men to unearth that little wizened body and its mother, or how shaken a non-medical man would be to witness such a gruesome autopsy. I wonder too if the specter of my ancestor's humiliation and subsequent years of hardship may have influenced two of the next three generations of Littles to become physicians – each with the given name David, until my grandfather Seelye's time. It is certainly a tale of mystery, love, and professional rectitude.

After uncovering and analyzing the "proof," Dr. Little knew the phenomenon of the stone baby was medically significant, and he made sure the exhumed artifact eventually found its way, tagged and preserved, to the New York State Historical Association Facility in Cooperstown, but this was carried out much later and not before he had fulfilled his promise. Shortly after the daring grave robbery, the doctor had shown the tiny grandbaby-corpse to his stricken ex-friend, firmly assuring him the cruel secret of this pregnancy gone wrong would never be publicly exposed until its memory was long outlived. With the restored admiration of one of the most prominent men in town, my ancestor was eventually able to regain his standing in their community and resume his life's work.

The old Chamberlin House on Plymouth had mysteries of its own, and two are notable. Ann was routinely pranked by her older brothers, Bill and Jim, by being taken down into the basement, which was once used as part of the Underground Railroad system. There she was told ghost stories about the slaves that "died" there. She would later cite these sessions as the cause of her becoming forever phobic towards mice and rats, describing a thrill of fear whenever she heard their scratchy feet running low between the hollow double walls of her old home.

Several cellars in Rochester's Old Town Inner Loop had been used in a neighborhood collaboration to hide runaway slaves in the early 1800s. The corner location of the Chamberlin place was strategically poised over a "depot," where two underground connections began in its catacomb-like cellar.

PAGE 23
Tuesday, July 18, 1961

Children See Where Slaves Hid

Museum Tour Visits Escape Tunnels

Rochester's role in the Underground Railroad came alive today for children in the Rochester Museum summer program as they wandered through Third Ward catacombs which reportedly sheltered slaves a century ago.

The honeycomb basement "depot" of the railroad is in the Saxton Apartment House, Troup Street and Plymouth Avenue S., along the Inner Loop.

Here, according to bits and pieces of history, slaves on their way to Canada entered by way of two tunnels and slept on stone platforms. One tunnel to the east apparently went to the Genesee River a quarter mile away. The other went through the rear of the house to wagons bound for Charlotte and ships to freedom.

The 8 by 20-foot cellar of stone and brick now can be reached from the main cellar but once was closed off and could be entered only by tunnel or by a trap door.

Thomas C. Montgomery, an attorney, lived in the house, formerly No. 59 South Sophia St. (named after Nathaniel Rochester's wife) from 1849 to 1855. Formerly the building was the site of the Atkinson Female Seminary.

HISTORIC 'DEPOT' on the Underground Railroad is viewed by two youngsters on today's Rochester Museum tour in the honeycomb basement of a Troup Street house.

Rochester newspaper clipping of the cellar of the Plymouth and Troup house, which was part of the Underground Railroad

One led toward the east, opening in a quarter mile to the Genesee River. From there fugitives could make their way north to Canada and freedom. The other route, tunneling away from the back of the house, ended where shipping merchandise was stockpiled. Here slaves hid in big containers and were loaded onto covered wagons headed for various ports unknown.

I doubt anyone had ever perished in my mother's cellar, but it was still a dangerous and ghastly journey for those people who penned themselves up in that tomblike shelter, sleeping on stone platforms in the dark. The idea of haints in that gloomy, dank, shadowy place was practically made for tormenting an intrepid little sister.

The other interesting episode in the history of the Chamberlin House came later, in the mid-1800s, and could be described as "The Reign of the Fox Sisters." Two of three sisters had been forced to move from their home in Arcadia, New York, in order to escape their neighbors' scrutiny. The sisters, Margaret and Kate, who held themselves out as spiritual conduits, generated such troubling rumors of strange happenings and suspicious activities that the township of Hydesville, New York, became convinced a murder had taken place in the Fox home. The sisters feared arrest and fled to Rochester. The women found rooms at the Chamberlin House where they continued with their mischief and incantation rites.

They ultimately gained acceptance into a radical Quaker sect already established there, and within this circle of "authenticity" the sisters soon gathered fame for their séances. They hosted "intelligent and morbidly curious" patrons and "those seeking communications with the other world."

Somehow this setup became so popular that people from everywhere

The Fox sisters

came to see them for consultations. I am sure my mother told me the Queen of England once went to visit the Fox sisters at the old house on Plymouth Avenue. I haven't been able to confirm that Herself came, but today the then famous sisters are credited with the beginnings of the Spiritualist Movement, which included European believers from "across the pond," so it is possible that a royal visit did occur.

Just the least amount of research will show how the duplicitous pair, Margaret and Kate, were convincing fakes. One of them used her knee bones to create loud thumpings in answer to all manner of esoteric questions on the supernatural. The Fox sisters were celebrities and hobnobbed in the swirl of skepticism, politics, women's rights, abolitionism, and temperance battles which marked that historically rich era.

When Kate Fox later confessed to the subterfuge, it didn't matter. The Spiritualist faith-train had already left the station, and many of the people on it continued to believe religiously in communication with the afterworld, forming Spiritualist Churches and the related nonprofit Spiritist Centers worldwide. Though the defamed Fox sisters died in poverty, the movement they helped initiate still rolls on — now bigger than ever.

SO LONELY . . . This house at corner of Troup Street and Plymouth Avenue South, once home to a female seminary, a group of spirit rappers, and underground railroad, now stands in gray and faded dignity as apartment house.

Newspaper clipping of the old Chamberlin House,
where Ann Little grew up

Chapter 10

FAREWELLS AND EUROPEAN GARDENS

The old Chamberlin House lumbered on into the 20th century and, with the advent of automobiles, witnessed a steady increase of accidents on its corner, many producing instant clientele for Dr. Little, whose clinic windows faced both streets. The doctor was privy to the brutal effects of many spectacular entanglements between the old-fashioned carriages and the new horseless ones. On one particular day, as he looked through his window, he was startled to see Ann lying face down on the cobblestones. She was midway at the intersection of the two roads, and he knew it was the most dangerous place on the street she

could be. Alarmed, he shot out of his chair and called out, only to see her head snap up to look back at him with a wide grin. She was doing it on purpose.

Angry, he brought her inside to his office and, making eye contact, he solemnly seated himself behind his desk, as if she were one of his patients. Instead of confronting or accusing her, he surprised her by saying, "That was a very brave thing you just did." Some kid had goaded her into it and she was busy explaining herself, but stopped when she heard him say that. Having gained her attention, her father counseled, "You would have been much braver to ignore that dangerous entreaty — you are old enough by now to appreciate the many varieties of courage." This new credo sounded smart to Ann, but she still wondered how hard it would be to refuse a really good dare.

Ann Little at camp with a friend

Ann Little would remember her early life nostalgically as carefree rambles with her doggie Toqué in the streets of Rochester, playing in the Big Woods near Alouette or paddling in Lake Ontario while her older brothers tinkered with their sailboats. She also recalled riding the railway filled with girls to Camp Nobscussett, near Cape Cod, where she learned to play tennis and swim using real strokes.

But then things began to change. By the time Ann was in fourth grade at the Columbia Prep School, she was struggling scholastically and beginning to feel inferior to the challenge. It was suggested by the headmaster that she repeat a grade. To make it worse, her sister Jane had attended the same school five years earlier and had done remarkably well.

But then her smarter, more popular big sister was in an automobile accident and, though the collision was relatively minor, the circumstances were questionable. Aunt Jane, at age 16, was arm-linked between two boys in the backseat of a newfangled car when the driver crashed into a concrete "dummy policeman" in the median. It ended in a hard ricochet back onto a high curb. It was 1:00 in the morning and her ribs were broken on both sides from two pointy elbows. Her physician father commented he had "never seen a young lady get three ribs broken by two gentlemen at the same time." Horrified, Mama Lit bolted into action.

By then brothers Bill and Jim were already in college and fairly autonomous, so the girls at home were Mama Lit's primary concern. The combination of Ann's poor grade reports and Jane's nighttime activities sent her into a flurry of planning. A continental trip abroad was in the works for a timely intervention. At 11 years old Ann was very interested in taking a good hard look at those nude statues she had seen in her textbooks, so she was all-in to go. Jane had little to say in the matter, as her midnight outings had precluded any objections.

With the underlying intent of exposing Jane to a society other than that to be found in Rochester, Mama Lit ostensibly planned the trip to teach the girls French, along with finding inspirational scenery for Jane and herself to paint. As a further incentive, the trip could also include a stop in Switzerland for a reunion with Betty Farley, Jane's best friend. This worked for both girls since Betty was a constant playmate for Ann as well as Jane during the summertime. The Farley family lived next door to Alouette on Lake Ontario, and they had both been missing Betty ever since she had left them for her European schooling the previous fall.

On November 4th, 1926, Ann turned the awkward age of 12 on the "one cabin class" ocean liner, the S.S. de Grass. The ship was heralded as an "Innovation in Economic Travel" where one could "Go to Europe in Comfort at Small Expense." There was a minimum fare of $120.00, calculated "by-the-room," instead of having to purchase an entire suite. A "single" was just affordable enough for Dr. Lit to agree to, though he probably held little sway over Mama Lit, an empowered woman with some family resources of her own.

Mama Lit in foreground, looking to be 50ish; note on the back reads "Mary Dodds Little on board ship someplace with some new found friends."

Ann was at that age when she considered being obnoxious a form of cuteness. In port at the harbor, after their long trans-Atlantic voyage, she rushed the dock by slithering through the disembarking crowd and ran down the gangplank, arms flailing high, shouting "I'm the first to set foot in the land of France." She would repeat variations of this horrid routine all along the trip, much to the exasperation of Aunt Jane and Mama Lit.

The next step was to enroll the girls in a Parisian public school to learn French while living in the Hotel Malesherbes, downtown near the Champs-Elysées. Uninhibited Ann began soaking up the local patois quickly as she made friends by teaching wild American games like "crack the whip" and "dodge ball" to her French schoolmates at recess.

Sophisticated Jane was mortified by Ann's behavior and reluctant to put herself out there, feeling withdrawn and missing her chums back home. The primary social activity, other than school, was when the three Little women would frequent the Luxembourg Gardens.

Mama Lit and Jane would set up easels to paint the fully-clothed statues of French queens lining the esplanade, but stop at different points along the way where they would have lively discussions with other artists or patrons of the park. The grownup talk bored Ann, but she made her own fun by darting about, rolling hoops with a stick, watching the Punch and Judy puppet shows, or floating toy boats in the garden's pools. The sisters were each getting their introduction to the greater world outside of New York, but Jane's command of the French language was not taking hold as her mother had hoped, so other options were being considered.

That Christmas Ann was surprised with one of her most memorable gifts. It was a box of Shredded Wheat, her favorite cereal from across the Atlantic. Unfortunately she immediately developed a bout of acute homesickness which only passed as they left Paris to push on toward Switzerland and the much anticipated visit with Betty Farley.

En route Ann thoroughly explored each of the passenger cars on their train and presently stationed herself, poised mid-aisle, as they prepared to stop for the necessary paperwork between countries. Ever the *l'enfant terrible,* she jumped out of the car onto the ground yelling, "I am the first in the land of Switzerland." Her mother and sister looked out vacantly from their seats, passports in hand, determined to ignore Ann's increasing lack of self-discipline.

Ann Little in Lausanne, 1926, age 12

After arriving in Lausanne, where Betty attended the international *Pensionnat Roseneck* for women, Mama Lit hatched a new plan. During their visit, she had observed that although few of the 20 plus students spoke the same native language, they had formed a tight comradery by trading their girlish secrets in the common tongue of conversational French. This was proof enough of the school's merit, so Ann and Jane were immediately enrolled. Ann's grades flourished under the close regimentation of enforced routine, while Jane was delighted to be back with her old pal "Bet" and found hilarity in this animated group of young women.

This situation lasted until Easter, when the entire school was let out for the students to tour Italy. For financial reasons, Mama Lit decided they should travel on their own. They took a train through the Alps to reach Italy on the other side of the 64,600 foot long Simplon Tunnel. At the mouth of the tunnel, Ann slammed their window shut as gusts of engine smoke sucked in, leaving sunlight behind in a fog of choking soot. At the appropriate moment, when exiting the cave-like darkness, an "I am the first to arrive..." must have been again enacted and tolerated. By mutual consent Ann was put in charge of working the windows down and up at each of the subsequently frequent tunnels. It kept her busy, though not silent. The only grace being given was the splendid landscape of Northern Italy sliding by, in between window-banging tunnels, as they clickity-clacked onwards.

Simplon Tunnel, 1914

At their first stop, Ann was properly impressed with the huge gothic Cathedral of Milan, which took mankind almost six centuries to build. She raced into its jumble of seemingly random spires, which magically coalesced into geometric symmetry as she bounded up the stairs, two at a time, to view the impressive architecture from above.

Next was Venice, where Ann got into a snorting fit of tearful laughter by leaping from train to boat in one quick beat. Somehow the act of it took hold of her, as her body tried vainly to adjust to the opposite rhythms of rail and water. She could not stop the laughing. When she caught her breath and calmed down enough to look around, she pleased herself by pointing, miming and using barely enough mock-Italian to buy one of the flat straw hats off the gondolier who was poling them through the canal passages. Next they traveled on to Florence, where Ann posted a letter to her father that became legend.

Jane had been invited to go "Tea Dancing" in one of the nicer Florentine hotels by a fellow traveler she had previously known in Rochester. He was there on vacation from Cambridge University and a nice enough fellow, but Mama Lit would only let her 16-year-old daughter be escorted by a college man if she herself went along as chaperone, which she did. As she left her younger daughter alone in the pensione she cautioned, "Now don't go and order any tea. It will cost extra."

After Mama Lit and Jane left, Ann got mad and tromped outside to pen a letter to her father, solo in Rochester with only Toqué for company, writing that she had been deserted and was "all alone in an Italian garden with nothing to eat and nothing to do, while Mother and Jane are out Tea Dancing. You can see the marks my tears are leaving on this page as I cry...." And so on and so forth. It was a priceless piece of self-pity and was to become a standard family "poke" at anyone wallowing in such a state of personal hyperbolic wretchedness.

When they got to Rome Ann saw a bit of the marble nudity she was so intensely curious about. In the early 1900s, attitudes were quite formal towards children and thus my mother had only seen fully dressed adults, including her parents, and had never viewed her brothers naked. Even nightclothes were considered private. This fascination with the unknown was only natural, but she evidently embarrassed herself, and more especially embarrassed her big sister, with noisy exuberance in many rarified settings by pointing and giggling while holding her hand over her mouth with dramatic gestures, as she hopped from foot to foot. The more uncomfortable her sister got, trying to look at nude statues of men with the aloof air of an artist, the more Ann hammed it up.

Sometimes the roles got reversed, as in the cathedral of "St. Paul Without-the-Walls" (meaning "outside the city"). Here Ann found the intricate alabaster windows a treasured delight and became transfixed in quiet reverie under their soft undulating light, until Mama Lit, nonplussed at her daughter's unaccustomed calm, broke in with, "These different kinds of marble remind me of various cuts of meat." And on it went.

As Ann continued sightseeing gardens, cathedrals, museums and the like, she began to feel adrift. When the proposition of returning alone to Lausanne to finish the school year was offered to her by Mama Lit, she wasn't hesitant. Along the way her age and temperament had been in irritating contrast to her sister's. She had slowly become aware that she felt no real interest in the gaggle of compatriots the two artists had assembled around themselves. Ann had loved her life at the Swiss boarding school and missed waking up to the snowy Alps across the lake from her dormitory room. She didn't mind when the two wanted to wander about in Italy and paint without her. She actually looked forward to some time without them, and these feelings puzzled her.

Unbeknownst to Ann, the pitiful letter she had posted to her father had found its mark and result-ed in a stern response coming straight back across the Atlan-tic, from Dr. Lit to Mrs. Dr. Lit, rebuking his wife for abandon-ing their younger daughter. Ul-timately this ended the Italian sabbatical for the two artists as they quickly rejoined Ann in Switzerland.

Mama Lit was grumpy about being reprimanded, and the "Italian Garden" let-ter gained a new wrinkle. The prized insider joke for the whole family became a stand-in for "party pooper" as well as an example of being a whiny poor sport.

The three women would be gone from their home for the better part of a year as Dr. Lit dutifully took care of business, alone in the Chamberlin House.

Jane Little, friend Dan Waterman, and Mary Dodds Little, near Paris during Ann's first European trip, 1927

Chapter 11

ANN LITTLE'S COMING OF AGE

When the family came back together in Rochester, it was decided that Ann and Jane should matriculate to the British Strachan School (BSS) in Toronto and prepare for college. It was there in Canada that my mother again found the predictability of routine. Just as in Camp Nobscussett, the Parisian Public School, and the Swiss *Pensionnat Roseneck,* Ann now understood that she thrived in a structured lifestyle. As a bonus, the gothic Canadian building of the BSS was within blocks of Lake Ontario, just 175 miles from Rochester, and comfortably across a lake, as opposed to an ocean, from home. There are many letters from Dr. Lit to Ann during this period of her life, from age 13 to 16. Toqué's patrols while making his rounds from the Chamberlin House to 162 Plymouth (his territory too) are as much a feature of this correspondence as the growing maturity evidenced in the return letters from my mother. She was passing into womanhood.

During holiday breaks, Ann would join the social festivities of her hometown by attending dinner parties and dances, but she always looked forward to the seasonal "coming out" balls. Her two older brothers, Bill and Jim, were typically included to round out the "stag line," formulating the all-important male-heavy ratio of guys to gals. This ensured all debutantes, winsome or not, had plenty of dance partners.

The "debs" were from the well moneyed families of Rochester, including owners of such enterprises as French & Co. spices, Bausch and Lomb eyewear, Hicky Freeman clothiers and Stromberg Carlson electronics. Many of the gatherings were exclusive, but since Jane was part of the popular clique, she always had more than one escort waiting for her to be available. Younger Ann, still away at BSS, could only make the "list" by tagging along with one of her three older siblings.

Looking the part was important, so Jane and Ann had to wear different evening gowns every night. These were provided by their wealthy benefactors, the Gordons – both clients of Dr. Little and close family friends. There was always big anticipation at the Chamberlin House when the chauffeur dropped off boxes of beautiful dresses from the Gordon girls, Cici and Lolly. These lovely clothes, recently cleaned and wrapped in fine tissue, came with dyed-to-match shoes in addition to dozens of silk stockings, little beaded purses and over-the-elbow kidskin gloves. They were last year's spoils, but Ann and Jane could not have cared less.

Ann knew the rules. The first dance was always with your dinner partner and you had to dance with him until someone else "cut in." This system could turn into a real horror. If no one broke in, you were stuck going round and round the ballroom floor with the same person, eventually having to excuse yourself for the powder room to join the other wallflowers-in-hiding. It was not such a bad place, with a chaise lounge, powders, rouges, perfumes, speculative chitchat...but still, it wasn't where you wanted to be either. Lucky for Ann, her older brothers rarely let this happen and watched her face whenever she danced by for any sign of tension.

Bill and Jim were on the other side of this convention, and Jim talked of being bribed to take on an unwanted dancer as her date flashed money out, behind her back, as they circled by. Unlucky girls had tricks of their own, using breakaway necklaces that could slip off their necks to crash on the floor, thereby creating a space for themselves in the river of couples. Here they might negotiate a better situation as passing dancers dropped to their knees in search of rolling beads. Adroit creativity was essential and pairing up with the one you wanted was always at stake.

Ann remained in her boarding school in Canada, and on the outskirts of her sister's social circle, until just turning 17 her senior year, when she opted out and returned to Rochester for tutoring in French, Latin, Algebra, Geometry, and Civics. These academic credits were all she needed to earn the last half point before entering William Smith College. It was 1931 and the recession, which had begun in 1929, was slowly dragging the industrialized world into the Great Depression. Everyone was feeling its effects, and the Littles were forced to let out most of the Chamberlin House in order to create another income stream to support the family. Mama Lit, Jane and Ann were relegated to the biggest of the three spacious attics until the economy got better.

The only exception was the suite of

Alice Owens Little (Topsy) surrounded by her four brothers; Seelye Little is front left.

corner rooms on the first floor where Dr. Lit slept and maintained his practice, complete with an adjoining room for his office and extra beds for the boys when they came home on visits. Mama Lit and Dr. Lit had always kept separate quarters, even at Alouette, so this wasn't as unusual an arrangement as it may seem. Even after the economy began to repair, the enormous old house would always have rooms to rent, becoming known as The Saxon Apartments, and would eventually be required to have two separate street numbers assigned by the city of Rochester. Regardless of their fractured living arrangements, the family continued to take their meals together, most often up the street at 162 Plymouth, with Aunt Topsy, Dr. Lit's sister and my namesake, Alice Owens Little, who lived there.

Aunt Topsy's 162 Plymouth Avenue dining room

The tradition of dining at 162 began very early on in the Littles' romance, starting before they were married, and continuing as their living and loving arrangements evolved. Mama Lit was never known for preparing regular meals and then even less so while she, Jane and Ann were holed up and living in the four room attic space, up steep narrow stairs at the top of the Chamberlin House. Typically, on those occasions when the family all sat down to dine at Aunt Topsy's, Mama Lit would critique the food being served and give Miss Mattie, the obliging cook, elaborate "pointers" on how things should be done. It was a formal table and everyone was supposed to wear nice clothes, use good manners, and come with "something interesting to say."

I have a picture of this dining room and in it you can see the portrait of my great-great-grandmother, Ann Eliza Owens (Livingston), hanging on the wall as it does in my own dining room today. The painting was done in the early 1800s, reportedly by an unknown New Orleans artist who went door-to-door selling framed, headless, busty, feminine torsos set against idyllic backgrounds. When a deal was struck, the lady of the house would sit for the artist and a likeness would be applied to the empty oval over the neck. The odd visage of my "great-great" with that crazy shoulder-breast combo surrounded by her overwrought, gilded frame certainly displays the power of heredity. In it an aquiline nose appears so fully realized that it was passed on to the next four generations; her daughter "Gus-Gus" (Catharine Augusta Livingston Little, and my sister's namesake), Dr. Lit, my mother and I all share that singular facial ornament.

Eliza Owens Livingston,
artist unknown

Ann Eliza Owens had come all the way from Limerick, Ireland, to marry my forebear, John Livingston, and he toasted her for taking his name at their marriage ceremony with "To my eternal love from the Emerald Islands, I present to all here gathered...my 'living stone.'" Sweet! And a good play on words. I guess the nose didn't put him off, inasmuch as his own was of a similar shape and length. I refer to it as the "Livingston Nose," in deference to this illustrious branch on my mother's side of the family tree, by way of Philip Livingston, who was among the 56 founding fathers to sign the Declaration of Independence and therefore a "point of pride."

"We always ate dinners with Aunt Topsy," was the way I heard it. As it turns out, I think Aunt Topsy was the heart of the Little tribe and everyone's go-to person for meals, advice, interesting repartee, and such as that. I also believe my mother was closer to her than she was to her own mother by that time. Aunt Topsy was so named after a character in the groundbreaking bestseller of an earlier decade, *Uncle Tom's Cabin*. The Topsy in the book was a young black slave and her description the exact opposite of my great aunt, whose eyes were pale blue (though round) and her hair white (though kinky).

If Aunt Topsy was the "heart," then her brother Dr. Lit was the "clown" of the family and I suspect it was he who anointed her "Little Topsy" as a child. He was 11 years old when she was born and the reference was supposed to be funny, notably because certain aspects of the character's personality were totally apt. Aunt Topsy was a tenacious little girl. She had to be, with a brother like Seelye Little – it was scandalous of him to make light of that serious book. Despite the old-fashioned maudlin tone, the work was an early effort to expose the horrors of slavery, and the plucky Topsy character was a central protagonist. Her brother's teasing name stuck and Miss Alice Little introduced herself as Topsy until she died at age 90.

Aunt Topsy never married; she was an "old maid," a virgin, and therefore stayed on at the 162 location as daughter and then caretaker of her mother, GusGus, who lived till age 88 and died at home in 1929. The role of family caretaker commonly fell to a girl or the youngest child, and she was both. Though Tops had suitors, and I am in possession of the proof in a love letter or two, she undoubtedly felt the constraints of this unwritten law. She embraced her spinsterhood with equanimity and humor, creating another kind of family as the long-time director of the Girl Scouts of America in Rochester and enjoying rich outdoor adventures with many friends alongside her in a lifetime of civic good-works.

I once visited my great aunt Tops in Cherry Valley, NY, where she spent her last years. She had converted an old barn into a home and crowned it "Rampage." That was a fit name for a place navigated by ramps, but also conveys the brilliant soul of the woman. Aunt Topsy had filled Rampage with antiques and curiosities from her long, eccentric life. I slept in the mezzanine, former hayloft area, which looked down into the living, former tack-room area, which sported matching ramps on either side of a big central fireplace. The two ramps led up to a long galley kitchen, former horse-stall area. It was clever and "primitive," before primitive was cool. She was old, but fun. Enchanted, I responded to her persona just as many young women had before me. She was into girl-power, and I can't imagine a more archetypical New Englander than she to be a mentor and stand-in mother for Ann Little.

Ann Little and her grandmother, Catharine Augusta Livingston (Little), also known as "GusGus"

In 1932, after leaving boarding school, mother smelled a rat in her dormered bedroom overlooking the corner of Plymouth and Troup (the same attic room that would be engulfed in flames within a de-

Rampage, 2014; photo: Henry Little

cade). She knew intuitively the sweet trashy odor's source was the same rodent that ran along inside the double walls of the old house. She viscerally understood the adage "I smell a rat!" and promptly packed her things to move up the street and await college with Aunt Topsy. Toqué was elderly and already favored the more comfortable 162 Plymouth Avenue domicile, so he moved in too. Ann's mother and Jane remained in the upper story of the Chamberlin House, and Dr. Lit continued to sleep in his ground-floor office suite. Ann was looking forward to going to a co-ed school and felt sure she would never return to Plymouth Avenue or that life again.

PART TWO

THE YEARS LEADING UP TO THE WAR

Chapter 12

WINNING AND LOSING ARE
NOT THE SAME THING

When Jim Tipton went to play football for Alabama, the athletic director was the legendary Coach Hank Crisp. Hank called his players "Piss-ants," with equal shares of affection and threat. He was known for his tough love. Jim had left one strict paternal figure only to find another waiting for him in the locker room. He fell right in line. Alabama's soon to be famous coach, Paul "Bear" Bryant, was still playing on the team as an end during my father's first year. In an account written years later, "The Bear" remarked that "Jim Tipton was my favorite scrimmage partner, rough as a cob!" He must have been — after all he'd stood his ground with Dr. Tipton so he could play ball.

My father was a fair to middling artist with a recognizable style. He made a scrapbook for his football years decorated with a cartoonish rodeo star burned into the wooden cover. I love showing it to people. Inside are glamour poses of him in his football gear and they always get a reaction. The man was movie-star handsome. The book also contains pictures of his ROTC group wearing nothing but underclothes and lolling about on cots in military tents, a group shot with his fraternity brothers in front of the Sigma Chi house and one interesting photo taken at the Warner Brothers Studio for the 1938 Tournament of Roses in Pasadena, California. He was being interviewed by a young TV newscaster, Ronald Reagan.

While away at college, Jim learned to stop relying on his little brother "Tip" to get dates. My uncle was as carefree as an autumn breeze on a hot summer day. Unlike my stand-offish father, he always had plenty of admirers and the girls seemed to pile up in drifts wherever he went. Back home, Tip had always been good about keeping his big brother fixed up with pretty gals for looming proms, dances, parties, etc., but now Jim found himself stepping up to that task and it proved to be much easier on his new campus than it had been in the past. Being on the A-team in a big university gave him instant popularity. All he had to do was show up and pick.

Though comfortable in the company of men, women and their girly ways baffled my father. He wasn't adept at flirtation, though he enjoyed it when the ladies came around, even more if they could carry on a one-sided conversation. Due to his height, he was in demand by the tall statuesque types. They knew they looked good hooked on his arm.

Clockwise from top left: Jim in ROTC uniform at the University of Alabama; Jim Tipton (fourth from left, third row down) and his fraternity brothers; Jim Tipton in Pasadena for the Rose Bowl, with young reporter Ronald Reagan; Jim as a tackle in his senior year, 1937 (helmets in those days were made only of thick leather, so a curly pompadour was often grown for extra cushioning);Jim in ROTC uniform at the University of Alabama; Jim Tipton in football gear, 1935, his sophomore year

His best secret weapon, other than the superhero looks, was his sense of rhythm. He was a natural born dancer and that seemed to satisfy his dates just fine, since lighthearted banter wasn't his strength. He loved the big band sound and his all-time favorite song was Hoagie Carmichael's *Stardust*.

Among my mother's effects I found an unusually long letter written by a young Jim Tipton to his family when he was away at college. It was dated November 15, 1934, and she had singled it out as important by isolating it in a manila folder in her file drawer of things to keep. She had written "GOOD LETTER" in large print on the envelope. It had a 3-cent stamp and a 3-cent postage-due, probably because it was so bulky. Here is the first of several excerpts on various topics drawn from that letter:

Jim with a tall pretty woman on his arm. Jim was something over 6'2", but always maintained he was "only 6-2" — likely a subterfuge that had something to do with height restrictions for flying the U.S. military fighter aircraft of the time.

Walked into the Sigma Chi house last night returning from church. First thing I heard was that a freshman football player had been killed. His name was Spurling and he came from Opp Alabama. It knocked me off my feet. He stayed in the B.O. house on the floor above me. Great big, strapping, blond headed fellow. Always full of pep and ever had something to say. Doesn't seem possible that we will never hear this genial patter of his around the house. His roommate took it pretty hard. It seems Spurling stepped off the curb at the "Soup Store," [and] a car going at an unusual high speed dropped him, dragged him about thirty yards, and did not stop.

The roommate saw the entire happening, in fact Spurling was knocked up against his leg, and, yet, he cannot explain or see how it happened. Now my diagnosis is – fate. The more I think about it, the more I become a fatalist. After going entirely through a season of football down here, which carries more risks and possible dangers then we sometime imagine, he leaves by a way which, in comparison, we would say was a hundred or a thousand times safer.

Obviously this incident left a lasting impression. When I was growing up, our family was Episcopal, like my mother's family, and not Southern Baptist, like my father's. I think he saw religion as women's work and he went along with whatever. He seemed ambiguous about things he couldn't build, fix or manipulate. I got to know my father by working beside him on projects. He was more of a physical than cerebral entity in my life, and my opinions about him are based largely on his actions or reactions during our day to day lives, not on any deep conversations. He once asked me what I wanted to do with my life, and I simply burst into tears. He never tried that again. I was too overawed by him. He was intimidating, even when he was trying to be gentle with his foolish teenaged daughter.

The only theology I remember discussing with him was concerning our family pet. We were talking about the way dogs think and what their emotions might be. He explained that our dog didn't love us in the same sense we loved her. To our little black Cocker Spaniel, Poppy, we were God.

After coming to the conclusion that Spurling was predestined to die young, Jim goes on to muse about his own college football career in that same letter, the one my mother had so carefully saved:

One thing – they are getting shurrer [sic] and surer that we may get the invitation to the Rose bowl. I certainly would like the team to go but, personally, I hope they don't. Why? Because I won't go along this year…we red shirts will have to stay and practice with the varsity until they leave – about Dec. 20 or 25.

When he wrote this letter he was a sophomore and this is the year that school athletes majoring in a demanding field, like aeronautical engineering, were expected to sit out so they could complete their academic labs. It was called the 5-year plan. He continues:

I want to go in one of the next three years (if I'm good enough) and a trip this year might ruin the chances. O, well! Nothing can be definite yet. Team looking plenty good now. Blocking and running like piledrivers.

The letter goes on to worries about money. He lists expenses like $6.00 for discounted clothes and the purchase of his Corolla Yearbook picture, following with,

> Please don't be too good to me. If I'm spending too much or almost too much just tell me to "shut down." I should feel terribal [sic] if I thought ours was the case where a son is having plenty of money in college while his parents were sacrificing and scrimping at home. Your letter was too vague on that subject. Don't think you will hurt me or feel that "I want my son to have a good time while he can 'or sompin'," because my best time will be had if I know all of you [are] having one too and not "listening to the howling wolf" for my sake.

He closes this 10-page letter with thanks to his mother for sending cookies and then gives kudos to his little brother Tip, still at home in high school:

> Let me tell you son, you are lucky not only to play on a winning team but to have had at least one year of coaching that will mean something later.... Congrats on the honors, too, but don't let them get you down. They [honors] have never gotten anyone anything yet, except, in certain instances, an unbecoming case of egotism, conceit, or big headedness, or what you will. I had better come back there and bask in all little brother's light of glory. Might mean something other than cannon fodder then.... Tell everybody hullo for me. Give my love to grandmother if you see her. Richard, tell Cormie the team looks great and is "a rarin' to go to the coast."

> Lots of love, Jimmie

The sign-off to Uncle Tip is significant. My father was a grinder, working hard at life with grit and determination, while baby brother lived life as it came. I only got to know my uncle as a person in the last decade of his life, after my parents had passed away. He would answer the phone, "All right?" and thought just about everything was "Super!" He had a sunny way about him and was always carefully deferential when he spoke to me about his more famous older brother.

As I spent time with my uncle, I found out he had done a brief stint in medical school before signing on, in solidarity with my father, in the Army Air Corp as a bomber in the Pacific during WW2. He had probably been tapped by his parents as the obvious choice to follow in the family business of medicine, and I slowly came to understand why. He had been blessed with a great life-advantage. Tip received a few of the double-whammy memory/ ambidextrous genes that sometimes crop up in a Tipton. This was a puzzle piece of the relationship between the two brothers I never knew. It surprised me. My competitive father looked the part — tall, serious, able — while Uncle Tip preferred to coast along, supporting his big brother's plans and humble about his own unusual abilities, unlike Dr. Tipton, who forced everyone to experience his excessive mind.

The year Jim wrote that letter to his family, the Alabama football team went without him to the Rose Bowl and became the 1934 National Champions. Four years later my

Richard Tipton as a young man

father got his chance and played tackle in the game of a lifetime. He went to the Pasadena Rose Bowl his senior year, January, 1938, and with 90,000 fans in attendance — still the third best attended Crimson Tide bowl game ever played. To my father's unbelieving disappointment, they lost. He never stopped analyzing that game.

Chapter 13

AN ACE IN THE HOLE

Near the end of his senior year Jim applied for Flying Cadet status, one of 30,000 or more trying to get into that elite group. To date, his only flight had been in the back of a Navy amphibious aircraft on a field trip with his engineering class in Pensacola, Florida. Just as he hoped, the U.S. Army Air Corps offered him a seat in the 1939-A Class. His excellent performance in college had undeniably gotten their attention. This was his first chance to fly and so very tempting, but he rationally decided to finish his degree and joined the later 39-B Class instead. This decision changed everything. He earned that Aeronautical Engineering degree and began with a 2nd Lieutenant's reserve commission in the Corps of Engineers from his four years of ROTC, but this slight delay caused his life to take a left turn.

Jim took his primary flight courses at Randolph Field in Texas, where he was paired with pilots in monoplane BT-6s and soloed in bi-plane PT-3s or PT-13s. Next he took advanced classes at Kelly Field in San Antonio, 35 miles to the southwest. The three disciplines offered were Pursuit, Bombardment or Observation, each using different types of aircraft and no cross training. He fell in with Pursuit, which suited him because the planes were supposed to be faster. He mainly flew P-12s, but tried Seversky BT-8s and AT-6s as well. He could fly any type of aircraft they gave him, and he did it as easily as walking a dog.

On July 15, 1985, Major J.A. Katz interviewed my father for the USAF "Oral History" program. Its mission was "To collect, preserve, and disseminate the personal memories, reflections, and lessons offered by leaders of character from the U.S. Air Force Academy and the U.S. Air Force." I use the transcription of their exchange as one of my primary sources for this book.

On p. 11, my father describes flying a P-12, the open-air, canvas biplane which he trained on in Pursuit at Kelly Field:

[It] was a dreamboat as far as I was concerned...a little old stubby thing. You could sit in the cockpit and practically touch the wingtips with your hands sticking way out with your goggles on.

It had a huge radial engine in it, and the fellows used to say it was like holding on to a Howard Sparrow engine with a feather in your fanny and here you go. It was a lot of fun to fly because it was just as maneuverable as it could be, but slow as blazes.

When Jim Tipton and the rest of his graduating 39-B'ers were all trained up and ready to go, they crowded around a bulletin board in good-natured jostling to get their duty assignments. That's when my father's master plan stopped working. Things were heating up across the ocean and even though the United States wasn't involved in the war yet, Roosevelt knew there was legitimate concern that things could change.

The class of 39-B was chosen to "test the feasibility" of using their recent Randolph graduates as flight instructors. Until then, two years of tactical duty was considered a minimum to teach the basics, but the school decided to hold back 10 of their best pilots to use as primary trainers and the name James Baird Tipton was on the thumbtacked list. Jim was stunned. He read it three times before he could believe it. He wasn't going anywhere; he was being given a desk job after all. He watched as his classmates got their orders to fly the fast new fighter class planes, the P-38s and P-42s, in exotic places like the Philippines, while he was being ordered to stay stateside. He felt cheated.

The Air Corps Training Center requests the honor of your presence at the Graduation Exercises

Kelly Field, Texas, May 25, 1939

Aerial Review   Exercises
9:30 A.M.   Post Theater 10:45 A.M.

Invitation to 1939 graduation ceremony at Kelly Field

In his 1985 USAF "Oral History" (p. 16) he wrote about his service as a military flight instructor:

> I was a young kid, wasn't very smart, all beaten up with broken noses and football injuries. I was flying; I got plenty of flying time, for Pete's sake, but usually in the back seat with a silly cadet in front of me. This isn't what I was looking for.

Jim wanted to go on missions and be out of Training Command, but he was a solid pilot and knew every kind of aircraft they had. His knowledge was just too valuable to let him go. Without result, he tried getting reassigned for the next two years by volunteering for every post that came up on the job board. When one finally hit, he was so elated to be getting out that he went to Dallas to become the Air Corps "check pilot" before he completely figured out the parameters of the job.

By this time the country's military build-up was obvious and even though the higher-ups had pushed all basic training to Randolph, they needed more flyers. The solution was contracting privately owned air-fields to speed output. In 1939 the Texas school had graduated about 500 pilots per year; by 1943, with the help of the contract-fields, they would be up to more than ten times that. What he had hoped was the "big out" was really an "all the way in." He was hired to oversee, or be a "check," for a semi-civilian flight school initiative; he was made the boss, but he had to build it first.

In his 1982 memoir my father describes his years in Ballinger, Texas:

This punk 2nd Lieutenant built an airbase out of a cotton patch in West Texas as Air Corps Supervisor and Commanding Officer (the part he must not have read) of a primary flying school for 400 Flying Cadets – one hundred more than my class at Randolph Field when I entered training. The contrast is both incredible and ridiculous. The same was being duplicated many fold throughout the U.S. – chaotic in detail, magnificent overall. The job was being done because we didn't know it was impossible.

Portrait by Howard C. McCall of Captain James B. Tipton when he was Commanding Officer for the Air Corps Training Detachment, Bruce Field, Ballinger, Texas; the drawing was used in "The Cadet," the yearbook for the Class of 42-I.

Jim Tipton worked so hard at getting the operation up and running that he wasn't completely aware of the implications of these quickly multiplying schools. He had an airbase to build with only a handful of Army Corps regulars; they worked long, late hours every day to make that happen. The public/private aspect of the enterprise really bothered him. He took a disdainful view of the civilian side of things, but had to finesse the deal, since they were the ones who supplied the students. He saw the field owners getting rich by overcharging the government for supplies, and he would rile those profiteers when he didn't push through and graduate all the pilots in every class. If they weren't ready by military standards, they weren't ready by his.

In his 1982 memoir, Jim wrote:

> The training command I disliked with intensity; it was keeping me from tactical aircraft. But we probably got more flying time, albeit training aircraft, and were exposed to more skills on an accelerating basis, because training command expansion necessarily preceded all others.

> I had fought the battle of command in the turmoil of untidy expansion.

> I'm speaking of command experience, not skill necessarily. We were too young and inexperienced, time was too explosive and organizations too irregular for traditional executive development. There are no illusions about what happened then, we did the best we could and devil take the hindmost.

Jim heard about the attack on Pearl Harbor when he was up in a deer stand in Junction, Texas. In his 1985 "Oral History" (p. 17) he describes his reaction to the 1941 attack:

> It was a kind of shocker. Of course that made me even more anxious to get out of that doggoned Training Command.

These were frustrating days for Jim Tipton. After the declaration of war he grew a rangy beard of protest in direct violation of dress code. He was

Jim Tipton in Texas sporting a wooly beard to protest being kept out of combat while serving in Training Command

trying to use this military misdemeanor as a tool to get pulled out of Command and put into the overseas fray. I know he and his students practiced crazy maneuvers in planes, like rolls and loop-de-loops, because he told me about the moments of blackout right after going into a nose dive and the thrill of coming to, plummeting earthward, before pulling out of it close to the ground. If these antics stretched the limits of protocol, he was probably doing more things like that too. He was in escape mode.

In his 1982 memoir, Jim writes about getting deployed and leaving Ballinger:

> I didn't know General Barton K. Yount very well, but I have reserved the right to malign him all my days. Had I not gotten a regular Air Corps commission, had not General Arnold insisted that he release his regular officers who wanted to go to war, probably I would have remained in air training command to the bitter end. Such was the fate of several of my classmates. Yount was obstinate. He scheduled our transfers from his [unit] over a 12 month period. He kept me lingering for 7 months. It appears that my scheduled date to leave the command was sacrosanct no matter that virtually I was twiddling my thumbs in the meantime.

General Yount eventually took Jim out of training and put him down at Foster Field in Victoria, Texas, to "get some tactical time," which he had been craving. He checked out in the single engine P-40s, P-38s and P-47s, but refused to check out in the B-24, a big four engine bomber. He didn't want his records to show he could fly any kind of aircraft other than pursuit.

Jim's instincts were right. Early in 1943 he volunteered to escort a supply aircraft down through South America, across to Africa and then up. He had all his shots and was cleared to go overseas when the order came down – the war effort no longer required pursuit aircraft. At the time it was wrongly believed that the war in Europe was over. When he got an offer to be a ferry pilot from the commander of Air Transport, he reluctantly decided to go. It was better than nothing, he thought. It wasn't.

Jim described the experience like this in his "Oral History" (p. 24-26):

> Right! This was a four-engine, phooey! ...There was a first lieutenant...a little old dinky fellow, I bet he didn't weigh 120 pounds dripping wet. He was the pilot of that doggoned thing, and I was his co-pilot. I had never flown a four engine job in my life and

didn't want to, still don't. But anyhow, we took off in that thing
and I'll never forget it.... That thing was 20,000 pounds over-
weight. They crammed everything they could in it...because it
was going to India, the China-Burma theater, where they were
having all that trouble with the Japs.... We pushed the throttles
forward, and it was 30 minutes before the wheels started turning, no kidding. We both were pulling back on this stick as hard
as we could with our feet up on the instrument panel. I thought
we were going in the drink! It finally staggered up into the air....
I don't even remember how I got back.

In his 1982 memoir he remembered it this way:

Thousands of pounds of spare parts and ferry tanks overloaded
the [B-24] aircraft well beyond the T.O. [tactical operations]
max. It didn't fly, it wallowed halfway around the world. My first
and last duty with four engine aircraft.

Also in his 1982 memoir he claims:

Don't remember too much about Victoria Field. I remained un-
assigned doing odd jobs while awaiting orders for the big show....

I find that statement completely inaccurate since, despite thumb-
twiddling and few memories of those 7 months, he managed to get
married to a woman from Victoria. I think she worked at the airfield and
supposedly toyed with him on an office dare. She had a toddler and was
either a young divorcee or war-widow. My sister, Catharine, remembers
our father talking to her just once about a little step-daughter he had
before she was born.

We both remember the union being described by our mother as a
shotgun marriage, though it later turned out the woman was not pregnant. The ceremony was performed on October 14th, 1943, not long
before my father was unknowingly to leave Texas and join a combat-
ready outfit. I found his marriage certificate in my mother's file labeled
Vital Statistics. The woman's name was Ann Weaver and the wedding
vows were exchanged in Portageville, New Madrid County, Missouri by
a Justice of the Peace. She was 21 and he was 28, and I knew there had
to be pictures.

My father was a shutterbug, so I searched through many, many
black and white prints until I noticed a curious set of 10 1"x1" images
pasted to black construction paper in one of his mother's scrapbooks.
My grandparents looked young, so I guessed they were taken close

to the right timeframe. They were all set in the same shady backyard garden on the same day. A tiny woman appears in seven of the photos, informally dressed in a skirt and cardigan, smiling like she was asking a question.

I got excited – I wondered if I had found what I was looking for. I peeled the pictures off, one at a time, until I found a label. It was simply a date, October 14, 1943. Bingo! It was written in my grandmother's distinctive hand. The whole lot looks more like a casual get-together than a wedding party. In one photo Ann Weaver seems to be showing something on her left hand to a much older woman, possibly a grandmother, while leaning into a hug from another woman, likely her mom. The only shot including my father shows him towering over his new bride in a standard work uniform, with his parents on her other side. Dr. Tipton is in a three-piece suit and looks to be the fanciest dresser there. He always preferred the best of everything, including clothes.

The amazing part of my discovery was how Ann Weaver looks like a cute, perky, dimpled version of my mother, the next Ann that would be my father's wife. At first I was appalled. NOBODY had told me that part. The woman's close resemblance to my mother was unmistakable. When I showed the 10 little pictures to my sister, she had the same reaction. He had a type? When I showed them separately to each of my children, Sara first and then Tip, they both thought they were looking at a young Miss Annie. I had to rethink my father. I had to rethink my mother. Which came first, the woman or the type? I believe the affair primed him for my mother.

The wedding pictures were pasted in the scrapbook beside photos and newspaper clippings that Miss Hettie had kept about her son from football star to military man. When my mother flipped through the Tipton family album, not being able to see the date on the back, could she have made the same connection I did? Did my mother ever understand these little snapshots were of the look-alike other Ann? I think not. People rarely recognize themselves in other people.

Jim Tipton's orders to join the 366th fighter group came through in November. Apparently the war was still on. He left Victoria only weeks after the little 1"x1"s had been taken. He went to Richmond, Virginia, to help his new outfit pack up. He talks in his USAF "Oral History" (p. 28) about how he got an advantageous assignment by being in the right place at the right time:

As a matter of fact, Dyke Meyer [Colonel Dyke F.], commander of the 366th, told me [this story] later; that when I first arrived I met him at one of the warehouses, where they were packing

Telltale snapshots, one of them dated on the back, from Jim's informal first wedding to Ann Abshier Weaver

up a lot of uniforms or something. The enlisted chaps were going through the line picking up items issued for overseas. I was sitting there talking to Dyke and something happened. I don't know what it was; I can't remember. But according to Dyke, I walked up to this fellow, tapped him on the shoulder, made a remark or two and asked him to do something, which he did. Dyke said, "When you did that, I figured you were my boy because you seemed to know what you were doing." In other words, I didn't realize anything unusual happened at the time. I just walked in, and he was looking for somebody to take with him as his deputy commander, so there I was.

My father left for Europe on the 19th of December and he was delighted. It was wartime, he had gotten a choice promotion and he was destined to be a part of the biggest world event of his lifetime. He had everything he had ever wanted, but for his new young wife it was unbearable. She was being left behind.

Chapter 14

GETTING YOUR CHOPS AND
THE PLIGHT OF CLAMS

When her father and brother Bill dropped her off at William Smith College in Geneva, New York, Ann decided to do a makeover. Taking her cue from Aunt Jane and Mama Lit, she was determined to smile more, laugh more and be interested in whomever she was conversing with – regardless – acting like she was having the best time of her life. She already knew from her brothers that men, in general, enjoyed listening to themselves talk, so she tried on her new persona at the very first dance. She worked at being approachable and attentive with every comer as a way to "wield her womanly wiles," hoping it was a matter-of-fact way of being engaging to the opposite sex. It worked perfectly. She couldn't get around the dance floor once, before someone cut in and she sailed off with another man. Ann Little was a success!

She had a wonderful year feeling pretty and popular and interesting. Her travels gave her topics of conversation, and her athleticism made her a good partner for young men interested in her favorite game, tennis, as well as ice skating, swimming and other sporty activities. She even ventured out of her comfort range enough to be cast in a minor role in that year's student play. She was in! Soon she was dating a senior by the name of Roy Brown, her first grownup boyfriend. He was a Kappa Alpha man, as were Bill, Jim and Dr. Lit, and so a very acceptable match. She and Roy once held a kiss in the "rumble" seat of a 1931 Model A Ford from Geneva all the way to Alouette, about 50 miles.

Ann Little, "waiting for Roy," 1933

This was extremely daring, since, when mother told me about it, I was evidently supposed to be shocked (I kind of was). I have a picture of her looking demure – on the back of the photo she penciled, "Waiting for Roy Brown, summer of '33, Alouette."

The following September, when Ann should have been back in school, she was instead the maid of honor in her sister's wedding. Aunt Jane married Monty (Montague Burrell Phillips) from New Hampshire. He was a former Dartmouth man whose college roommate was Ted Geisel, later to become the famous "Dr. Seuss." The roommates were great party-goers and known to keep late hours. Monty quit college after his sophomore year to pursue some frothy redhead and this episode in his life was forever memorialized by Ted's drawing of "Lady Arabella Godiva – The Sleep-Walking One."

Uncle Monty eventually found himself, still a bachelor, working in a Rochester investment brokerage. Jane probably met her match at one of the many dances held at the Genesee Valley Club, where he was a member, or possibly in a less formal setting. I would guess the latter, since there is a sketch of the "Mechanized Clam," another Dr. Seuss original, drawn on the back of a dinner menu from the Country Club of Rochester.

Miss Jane Little, daughter of Dr. and Mrs. Seelye W Little of Plymouth Avenue South, whose engagement to Montague Burrell Phillips of East Avenue was announced yesterday.

Jane Chamberlain Little as a young woman

The venue was founded in 1895 as a casual "family club" for the "everyman" and is one of the oldest community golf courses in the U.S. Monty was enough of a regular there to bring his former roommate along – at least once. By reputation, anywhere Monty went a party surely followed, and that would have certainly included my fun-loving, Charleston dancing, witty Aunt Jane. My cousin Nick (Jane's firstborn) has both the clam and the forgotten Arabella framed and hanging on his walls today.

Along with her sister's marriage, there were several events taking place simultaneously that would change Ann's initial trajectory. The Great Depression was full on and taking its pound of flesh from everyone, while her father was having trouble with blood clotting in his legs and often unable to work. The resulting loss of income was ever tightening the squeeze on the Littles, so how to pay for Ann's tuition was an obvious concern. Besides, her grades had slipped, her beau had graduated, and she was over it. More to the point, she had just turned 20 and hadn't heard from Roy in a while. Whether Roy had found another girlfriend or was unemployed and had little to offer a bride, she felt pressure to get on with her life. Newly married Jane was vacating her employment at Lincoln Alliance Bank & Trust, and arranged for her younger sister to be her replacement. Ann leapt at the chance.

She began each day in the bank's basement, staffing the Safe-Deposit area. At 3:00 PM she was given 45 minutes to freshen-up before trudging to the top floor Transit Department. When the bank closed, she stayed upstairs at her desk until all credits and debits balanced for the day, sometimes at 5:00 and sometimes much later, then she went back downstairs to hop a streetcar. There were rarely seats and she usually stood, holding onto the overhead strap for every stop and start during the 30-minute ride back to Aunt Topsy's, where she would climb the stairs and collapse in a heap on her bed. Ann was young and could withstand the long hours, but the drudgery was unrelenting. Sometimes she would sneak a nap on the conference table in the booth reserved for bank customers. It was a secure, dimly lit space used by anxious patrons to retrieve dwindling holdings from the bank's vault, clipping their bond-coupons in private while the economic implosion raged on above them.

Miss Ann Little kept at her job for the next four years and it was during this time she got to know Anne Montignani and a whole new group of friends, including a bubbly girl named Susie Peck. Sue had the same birthday as Ann's older brother Bill and that tiny bit of coincidence produced an introduction. Before long the effervescent Sue had Bill doing things so uncharacteristic of him that the whole family knew he was getting serious about her. Horseback riding,

Bill Little as a young man

bridge playing, and dating were bewildering pastimes for the reticent Bill, an engineer and quiet hobbyist.

He was mercilessly kidded by brother Jim, especially since Sue was eight years younger and such an unabashed tease. I remember Aunt Sue being "scandalized" while peppering her conversations with interjections like "Oh my DEAR!" or "You're not SERIOUS!" all the while looking mock-horrified by whatever subject was in play. Aunt Sue was Uncle Bill's pure joy and forced him outside his shell.

Eventually first son Bill was happily married to his sweetheart and engineering Depression Era public works projects like parkways and dams, while second son Jim remained unmarried and heading up the corporate ladder at the Chamberlin Rubber Company (the Dodds' family business). When social events and holiday festivities rolled around, Ann was one of the few single working women still in their circle. Most of the female attendees were well-to-do, or otherwise taken care of and could sleep in. Not Ann. At night, her dancing feet hurt from standing, during the day her head hurt from going out. It was a noxious cycle of pain going from her feet to her head and back again.

Acting as both theorist and savior, Jim came up with a hopeful solution. He decided the real culprit of morning headaches was all the cigarettes they puffed away at and not all the grog they drank. All four siblings formed a pact; any time during any party, if caught smoking, the offender had to pay out $10.00 on the spot. This was not only embarrassing, but a lot of "moolah" during the difficult 1930s. They had some laughs with that "gotcha" plan, making a big show of it at family gatherings, but little sister Ann, the poorest of the four, made sure she never had to forfeit any money. I think that foresighted policy extended her life. She was forced into early self-control, and I cannot recall my mother ever smoking more than one cigarette, always a filterless Camel, at the end of each day. Eyes closed, in bed, she made it look delicious.

By early 1937 Dr. Lit was dead. His clots had become more and more disabling, leaving him bedridden and speechless from a series of strokes. It had been decided he should ride out the long ordeal in his boyhood home at 162 Plymouth, with his sister and Ann, who often kept him company after work by reading to him before going to sleep. Aunt Topsy, Mama Lit, Jane and Miss Mattie bustled around during the day, making sure he was fed and cared for. It was rough. When the misery was over, the house on Plymouth Avenue was closed up to be sold and by the following October all the women who had been attending their patriarch had scattered.

As domestic help, Miss Mattie began her well-earned retirement, while Dr. Lit's main caregiver, Aunt Topsy, at age 59, was freed of family responsibilities in ways she had never been in her entire life. She took an apartment in town and then proceeded to the Little ancestral seat in Cherry Valley to refurbish the old family barn with select antiques from 162 Plymouth Avenue, among them a patina-crackled drop-leaf breakfast table and a lady's writing desk that I now have in my home. As she lived her life, Aunt "Tops" traveled far afield, usually with small groups, and continued to enjoy hiking, camping and all the wild outdoors well into her later years.

She was the literate type too and stayed engaged in real-time happenings by keeping a wary eye on world events. She wrote well considered letters on notable issues until her death. In one such she holds forth:

> Nowhere in the world is there a talented group of men with as permanent and tight a hold on the reins of a great nation; as experienced in war, organization and travail; as devoted to their purposes; as capable in intrigue, propaganda and practical doctrine as is combined in the regime of the People's Republic of China under Mao Tse-Tung. It is a terrifying combination made even more frightening should the threat be largely ignored in deference to the comparatively well recognized and understood Soviet Spectre.

Wow! The address on the top of the monogrammed stationery is 41 North Goodman St., Rochester 7, and I have only a single piece of the letter, written longhand in ink, using numerous semicolons — no date, salutation, or closing — but obviously sent years after WW2 from her apartment in Rochester. No wonder my own dinnertime memories are full of political discussions and rivaling opinions. Sitting at the Ann and Jim Tipton family table, if the talk got heated, it was never vulgar, mean, or snarky. And you couldn't filibuster either. If one could not make a point using facts and persuasion, you were politely ignored. My parents typically nullified each other's votes in presidential elections. Jim to the left and Ann to the right.

Chapter 15

ANN'S SECOND EUROPEAN TOUR

As Aunt Topsy moved on, so did the other three Little women left in my grandfather's departing wake. Mama Lit repaired to Alouette to collect herself, Jane was busy with her first pregnancy and, using money from Dr. Lit's slim estate, it was decided that Ann should be given the chance to go back to school and finish college overseas. She quit her taxing job at the bank. It was time to catch a tailwind and sail back into life.

Mama Lit oversaw her daughter's "bon voyage" party. Ann wore her new navy-blue traveling suit with pink trim, and an old dowager well-wisher presented her with an orchid corsage to pin on the lapel. It was a big send-off. Even a photographer from the local paper was there to document her "grand" departure. Mama Lit had a hand in orchestrating the whole shebang and the underlying message being sent out to Rochester was that "the Littles are still here." The clipping from Rochester's society column is titled, "Will Continue Studies Abroad," and the caption reads:

> Miss Ann Little, the daughter of Mrs. Seelye Little of Lake Road, Webster, is pictured here on shipboard as she sailed Wednesday for France to spend a year studying at the Sorbonne in Paris.

Anne Montignani, Ann's friend from the bank, went with her on the S.S. Bremerhaven to a port in Germany on their way to Paris. Before they got to the "City of Light," they took a train to Cologne for a boat trip up the Rhine. The exquisite pastoral scene floating by was the inspired backdrop to display how far the two had come.

Newspaper clipping from Rochester's Democrat and Chronicle

With over two weeks en route, they felt like "world weary travelers" and gloried in how easily they had blended into the foreign crowd strolling along the deck of the river-cruiser. They had scraped off the "Baseball and Apple Pie" like so much provincial goo. Making no eye contact, they both struck a pose of highly affected nonchalance by languidly draping their bodies on the railing as they watched the shoreline slide away. Presently they spotted two handsome strangers in stylish trench coats coming their way, exotic young men who were titled Englishmen, or at the very least French.

One said, "American, right?" in a very familiar accent, then quickly, "I'm Marvin Rosenblatt and he's Larry Einhorn from Rochester, New York!" By the end of that simple introduction, the girls' pretense at European sophistication had devolved into self-conscious giggling. Unaware they had blown through the girls' cover, Marvin and Larry continued to hold forth, encouraged by such an easy-to-please audience. Everything they said got funnier and funnier to that silly pair, Anne and Ann. In fact, the girlfriends giggled all the way to Paris, delighted to find in each other a well suited traveling companion. Not always a sure thing in any relationship.

They were on their way to study *Civilization Française,* a joint interest since Miss Montignani had graduated from Mt. Holyoke in French Art and Literature, while Miss Little had graduated from nowhere, but spoke the language fluently. In truth, pursuing a degree was more of a lark, neither of them taking it too seriously. They were both 23, independent, and every so often, for no particular reason, Ann felt her blood flit through her veins at break-neck speed. She gloried in those ecstatic moments and gloried in her "joie de vivre."

The girls eventually arrived at the Sorbonne and settled into their new lodgings. By happenstance, the Paris Exposition had just been erected nearby and included an art exhibit that both Ann(e)s wanted to see. The charge for the show included touring the Expo, so they went there too. The outside was stunning and did not disappoint, although the inside was just as garish as Ann had suspected it would be, more like a carney sideshow back on New York's Coney Island than a world class tribute to Paris.

Since they had arrived in France the street-talk was all about the Expo, or the "Ex," making it sound like that was the only reason to even come to Paris in the first place. At the same time the city appeared to Ann both threadbare and tawdry, with military types roaming the streets and everywhere loud bombast over War versus Peace. Hadn't Europe just finished the war to end all wars? The impression was confusing; even the famous Papillon restaurant in Barbizon had closed.

During weekdays the girls took their lessons at the Sorbonne and every weekend they headed into town, typically retrieving their mail from American Express before going to galleries or that week's opera or show. Sightseeing by day, they gobbled up the night life too and continued with the giggling around stray male admirers. Ann even experienced an interesting tête-à-tête with a French girl named Gisele, who took her to an all-girl lesbian nightclub.... "Ooh La La!"

At some point Mama Lit came to visit. It was her plan to venture out from Alouette and trip from place to place in search of ambiance and better times, but to Ann her mother's surprise appearance was more like a surprise imposition. Her mother chided her that she had let herself get fat on French cuisine. She also complained about the city's loss of character, and very shortly left Paris for the south of France with some fly-by-night artist she met at the American Exchange. Ann had tried to be gracious towards her mother, allowing for her need to recover from the prolonged paralysis and death of her husband, but she and her friends were too involved in their own interests to give anyone else much attention. Mama Lit needed to discover a place she had never been before. Going to beaches in Nice was the better diversion for Ann's free-spirited mother.

At midterm, Ann and Anne decided to save the school's overblown sitting-fee by skipping final exams and instead used the money on a skiing adventure as a holiday present to themselves. They settled on Berwang, Austria, nestled high in the Zugspitze Mountain Arena. On a train, the first leg of the trip, they shared their compartment with three vacationing contemporaries who had brought goatskin flasks of wine to share. Tipsy, the girls crawled onto the overhead luggage racks for a fitful night facing each other across the car as they simultaneously rested and clung to narrow wooden slats, careful not to drop onto the sleepers below.

After the railway brought them as close as it could, the rest of the journey was accomplished with a tall sleigh pulled by an enormous draft horse. It was a surefooted beast and their only option of getting into the steep mountainous passes. Exhausted and excited, they arrived at their quaint hotel, tucked into an alpine valley, just in time for a picturesque Christmas Eve.

Their room was cozy-warm, with a frosty window overlooking the town square. In the soft twilight worshipers could be seen gliding in on skis, which they stowed upright in the drifts of snow before entering the bright indoors of the sanctuary. Ann fell asleep to faint strains of caroling as she burrowed deep into starched white linens encased in an eiderdown counterpane. She could hardly believe that only a few months ago she would have still been in lock-down, balancing debits against credits up high in a windowless cube.

Skiing was more than a winter sport for the locals, it was the fastest way to get around and soon the Rochester newbies had mastered the "stem curve" technique of "lean from the hill away," and kept their skis in a V for balance. When adept enough, they joined the graceful lines of cross-country skiers in the silent promenade known as "spatziergang." The tradition was a playful activity initiated whenever a group of people would cue up, one behind the other, and rhythmically move through the hills surrounding the village; anyone could join in or peel out at will.

The faster downhill runs proved more problematic than the slow promenade, and the Ann(e)s would often substitute the reliable "butt brake" technique for the V grip when whipping down a slope, out of control and in danger of plowing into fellow skiers. These were "high old times," where every day ended with beer, stein songs, more giggling and much lederhosen-slapping as they danced away their nights. It was a sublime two weeks never to be forgotten by my mother.

When they returned to Paris and the Sorbonne, a new arrival had checked into the pensione. He was a tall Swede named Sven Gunner Lindstrand, and Ann noticed a subtle exchange between him and Anne Montignani. She watched the appreciative return glances as the two did a double "look back" when they passed each other for the first time.

As for Ann's romantic interests, she was being monopolized by the son of the hostel's proprietor, Mademoiselle Coulet. His name was Sascha and he was a little too attentive. He shadowed her wherever she went and she could not lose the man. She described him in a letter she posted to Jane as "a pixie, very amusing and smelled of cheap French cigarettes." "It was a strangely childish affair," she continued, "in which he said hardly a thing," but his constant presence made it difficult for young Ann to meet any other men. In the meantime her former partner, the other Anne, was off spending most of her free time getting to know Sven.

If there had been an internet password in the 1930s with the security question, "what is the name of your first girlfriend," my mother's would have been "Anne Montignani." I feel sure she was Ann Little's first real love. It was the chaste, heartfelt kind of bond that sometimes happens in youthful innocence, but can leave behind a poignant mark all the same. She knew her friend wasn't pulling away from her, only moving beyond her and entering into a sphere of emotion Ann could not yet follow. If there was hurt or jealousy, those feelings were completely overwhelmed by their mutual affection. She wanted the best for Anne, and the best was to be loved.

In a letter to her brother Jim, dated March 1, 1938, Ann wrote:

And thinking thus of the future, visions of a ruined world flash through my brain. It doesn't seem as though this unsettled state could go on very long without the whole world going up in smoke, including that fortress of reliability and prestige, the Chamberlin Rubber Co. Honestly, if you could see the poverty and rottenness over here you'd wonder how anybody could pay for anything.

Germany looks richer than it is and France looks poorer than it is and neither one has what they want. Preparations for war, either military service or the manufacture of armaments, seem to keep everyone happy for the moment, but how long will it last?

The letter is a rambling nine-page missive and mostly about Ann's travel plans, her wayward mother and her diminishing funds. A war, much less a war that involved the U.S., was hardly a real possibility in my mother's mind, but there it was, tucked in towards the end of the letter...the unfinished business of Europe. The last page, at the bottom of her robin's-egg blue stationery, she closes with "Love from Ann" and then the postscript, "Dad was buried a year ago today."

Likely as not, she wrote this to her brother on that particular anniversary because, of all her siblings, he was most like their father, Dr. Lit, and she needed to vent. Jim was the self-appointed moral relativist and prankster of the family, as well as the acting president of the Chamberlin Rubber Company (since 1935). His skillful management would benefit all four of the Little children in future years, once the majority shares passed on to them, but at the time she just needed the assurance of him as a safety net for her feelings.

When I was nine, I attended a dressy Thanksgiving meal Uncle Jim was hosting. The extended Little family was there and I was the youngest of all the nieces and nephews and the only southerner from out-of-town, other than my older sister Catharine. I was anxious and gawky. It was a lovely spread with a delicate floral center-piece, fine china, cut crystal and a perplexing array of spoons, knives and forks at each place setting. During the meal, just at the time everyone had quieted down to feast in earnest, I dropped a large "something" onto my plate. Corncob? Utensil? At any rate, when it hit my cutlery and food with a loud SPLAT, the clatter got everyone's attention. I felt mortified under the polite titter of amusement as my throat constricted, burning to cry.

Uncle Jim, sitting at the head of the table, saw my embarrassment and locked eyes with me in sly conspiracy. He immediately grabbed all the silver from around his plate with both hands and flung it over his shoulders, never taking his eyes off mine. It made a huge racket when it hit the hard marble-tiled floor and the snickers from around the table instantly gave over to loud guffaws. Some of my cousins laughed so hard they cried. In one magnanimous gesture my uncle had switched off the formal atmosphere, relaxing his guests through my catharsis. This was classic Uncle Jim.

When the term ended for spring break, a previously planned girls-only trip on the continent was next on the agenda. Despite the heat rising up between Miss Montignani and Sven, the friends kept to their initial itinerary of retracing much of mother's tour of Italy with Mama Lit and Jane from a decade before. Before leaving Rochester they had made arrangements to stay their first week in the same pensione in Florence where Ann had lived as a youngster.

The place looked different, much smaller and not at all as Ann remembered it. The back courtyard, her "alone in an Italian Garden" spot, more closely matched her mind's eye, because of the leaf-filtered light and the soft earthy smells. She smiled ruefully thinking back on that dumb letter she had sent forever ago. She missed her daddy and wished she could still write him, tell him about her trip, about how grown up she was and how good her French had become. She laughed quietly when she remembered how he had once explained the correct way to pronounce au revoir, "Say it like you are gargling your own spit, Annie!" And she did.

The girls celebrated Good Friday by watching an outdoor rendition of *passione-di-cristo* where three actors were "crucified" on heavy wooden crosses after dragging them up a hill. The men were actually standing on unseen platforms, but they looked hung and dead with fake blood in all the right places. Next it was on to Easter Sunday and the uniquely Florentine *Scoppio del Carro,* or "explosion of the cart." The Ann(e)s linked arms, joining the fantastic parade of 15th-century pageantry led by a manicured team of white oxen with garlands of flowers twined through their horns. The team was pulling a 60-foot high, ca. 1622 cart filled with an arsenal of fireworks in honor of the first Christian Crusade. The girls joined the crowd at the main plaza, watching expectantly until a white dove was freed to the cheers of *Ecco! Ecco!* or "Look! Look!" Every child was held in the air to see it fly towards the cart.

The tension, conceived within a spectacle of religious imagery, comes to a thunderous climax as one little bird flaps its way across the courtyard from the huge cathedral towards the bell tower and explodes in a shower of blazing ritual. This annual Tuscan event, derived from an ancient rite to bring good harvests, is thought to go back as far as the mysterious Etruscans, a predawn civilization from that part of the world.

The ascension of a lone dove to fend off the worst possible scenario for hardworking farmers everywhere is a seductive visual of faith and hope...made even more impressive if you consider that birds are descendants of dinosaurs. Nowadays the celebrants see a fake, cruelty-free, mechanical dove "fly" down a zip-line to ignite the cart's lightshow. The symbolism still works.

It was a culture-packed two months and the final days of the girls' unique friendship. Amid picnics, museums and overland hikes, the secretly betrothed Miss Montignani kept herself busy with daily postings to Sven (replete with deep sighs and distant gazing), while Miss Little tried to keep bearings on her mother, still roaming around somewhere in southern France. Travel remained easy between the two Ann(e)s, even if the shared giggle fits were fewer and tapered off more quickly.

Back in New York, two curious Montignani sisters, Betty M. Guest and Jean M. Jenkins, were packing their steamer-trunks to cross the Atlantic on a mission to inspect their potential brother-in-law, the "Swede from Stockholm," before giving their sister an approval. Apparently he passed the familial scrutiny, since the couple's intentions were soon made public. After a month in Florence and a final whirlwind two weeks in Rome, Anne, Ann and everyone else they knew in Europe met back in Paris for a traditional Nordic engagement bash.

This is when my mother first heard the word "smorgasbord" and was introduced to Scandinavian hors d'oeuvres like raw fish, dense meatballs and pickled beets. She also mastered the Norwegian salute to good health: look at your drinking partner, get serious enough to totally focus on one another and shout "skol" as you both toss back a shot of spirits. In Ann Little's case this would be schnapps, since she didn't yet trust the vodka. The long initial stare was supposed to be an inherent test for relative sobriety and a good way to mitigate outright drunkenness — important during a festivity where drinking was to be expected. Sometimes the opposite happens and a shout of "skol" only starts more rounds of toasting and less seriousness, making the bleary-eyed exchanges between drinkers entirely moot.

On learning of the pending nuptials, Mama Lit had promptly hot-footed her way back to Paris, hoping for a raucous party, and was no doubt pleased to be with the cheering hometown group speculating on the upcoming "event." After all the celebrating was over, she took her slightly forlorn, weepy daughter on an extended tour of France by way of Normandy, and Miss Montignani left for the states to begin planning her lavish socialite wedding.

In a letter to her sister Jane, dated May 3, 1938, Ann Little wrote:

I suppose mother has told you that Anne Mont is engaged to a Swede – she told everyone over here, so I suppose it's all over Rochester by this time. Anyhow he is a very nice gent with what it takes to get ahead and she will be very happy. She likes the life over here and of course having plenty of money will always [help her] to keep her independence. On the whole a good set-up although she has never seen the young man's parents or the country in which she expects to live – Poor me! My heart is still in the same place and I guess I might as well give up and die.

The economy was such that Ann's year-long "studies abroad" adventure had cost $1,000.00 (the equivalent of $17,000.00 in 2017), including items she sent back as duty-free imports: Ratsie sails from England for Bill, Luneville china for Jane and some Quimper pottery from France for herself (which I display in a curio cabinet in my home). These three items represented the only tangibles remaining from her inheritance and any dreams she might have had of turning her future in a new di-rection. Though she had tightfisted her spending and meant to keep a little back for her return, she soon relented and wired Monty for her last $200.00. She needed to stay on with her mother and put off the gut-wrenching voyage home for a little while longer.

Ann Little returned to be a bridesmaid the following spring, June 2, 1939, along with Anne Montignani's three sisters, Betty, Jean and

Ann Montignani and Sven's wedding dinner; Ann Little seated at back left

Francis (her maid of honor). The expensive affair was big news in those dismal prewar years and the Rochester *Democrat & Chronicle* made the most of it with large photo spreads and long flowery descriptions of the ceremony. The couple soon moved away to distant Sweden and my mother wondered if she would ever see her bonne amie expatriate again. Throughout the rest of her life she would miss her friend Anne Montignani with a deep resolve, always citing their friendship for making her into a better person by trying to be worthy of it.

Chapter 16

THE WORKADAY WORLD AND BEYOND

After all the fanfare at her departure for Paris the year before, Ann now found herself back in Rochester, still single, with only a puny bit of cash and a few ceramics to add to her "hope chest." Even after many close encounters which might have ended in marital bliss, there were no obvious prospects for finding a true love. Her spirit was down and she winced at that silly girl dining alfresco in some balmy Italian café, sipping vermouth cassis, thinking smugly "am I the girl who slaved four years in a bank?" It was a hard truth.

By autumn Ann was trying to earn her keep by working on commission in a fancy dress store named "Helen Whitney Miller." It was conveniently located in nearby Brighton, where she could stay with Jane, Monty and her little nephew Nick, when not bedding down at Alouette. The shop specialized in evening wear and wedding dresses. Each time a customer would hail her as "Mam," in that specific way reserved only for underlings, it always made the hackles rise along the back of her neck. She got "Mammed" and "Miss Littled" to distraction trying to accommodate the so-called ladies, with their constant demands and trying hissy fits. She never forgot the dejection she felt while serving the public and was forever afterward kind to clerks, or anyone else who was trying to be helpful.

The dress shop was not good employment for Miss Little. She was too vain about not being vain. She wore makeup sparingly, if at all. She might put on a thin bit of lipstick and a dab of powder, only using a good hard pinch to the cheeks for color. She certainly did not have a natural savoir faire for fashion. Unlike Aunt Jane, who had a knack for understated flair, Ann could only muddle through. She put a high priority on sturdy, well-stitched clothing, obviously never cheap, but not necessarily flattering either. Whenever Ann stepped out in clothes that would set off her nice figure and pretty legs, it was usually by accident. She didn't dwell on being attractive so much as being appropriate. She worried most about not looking poor or crass. She didn't want to appear desperate.

When her old boss from the bank offered to rehire Ann, she was grateful. She returned to a predictable salary and continued working at a branch office issuing loans out on Exchange Street. After a couple of years she knew she needed more income and learned typing skills and the Gregg Shorthand system so she could try for a position with the federal government, one of the few places still offering opportunities during the Great Depression.

She applied to take a Civil Service Exam, which required her to bring her own equipment to the Post Office. She brought her steno pad, a typewriter she had rented for just one day and persuaded her would-be employers to let her borrow one of their portable tables. The typing went well, as she expected it would, but though good at puzzles and cryptograms, she felt insecure about her shorthand abilities. The woman dictating for her test used a sing-songy voice while reading the words in a dull, unnatural monotone. It threw her concentration off, so she wasn't too surprised when she didn't get a callback.

My mother was not the introspective sort. She liked to stay with the pack and though she wanted to be married with babies, she tried not to let herself worry about it either. She wanted to get the wedding thing right. Her feminine role-models spanned the spectrum from unmarried, but happy Aunt Topsy, to married and completely miserable Betty Farley — whose marriage was failing by the end of the 1930s.

Apparently Betty Farley had always been in love with the boy next door, Ann's brother Jim. Since the Farleys had a place adjacent to Alouette, the two families' children had all bonded during the warmest

Jim Little as a young man

months of childhood — long days full of endless play and summer intrigue. The Little family's household, with two boys and two girls, was the popular hangout and a second home for most of the neighborhood kids. Betty, a quick read, adored Jim Little for his priceless stunts. He was the leader of their summertime gang and she was his favorite co-conspirator when devising new plans for more fun.

In this era, in this part of the Western Hemisphere, it was expected that a young woman be married by her early 20s. When Miss Betty Farley reached that prime age of womanhood, she had plenty of reasons to stop waiting on her teenage crush, rascally Mr. Jim Little. He was on a slow burn, acquiring assets with the Chamberlin Rubber Company and playing the field as a man about town. She was in his group and she saw him around, but he was always kidding, hard to pin down and never gave her enough reliable encouragement to expect a real proposal.

At the time, Betty was being courted by another man. He was handsome and from a suitable family. Though eager for the next phase of her life to begin, she was hesitant, still hopefully waiting on Jim. The more she hesitated, however, the more determined her suitor became. She eventually opted into the marriage. From the outside they appeared to be a good fit. He was prosperous and she well cared for. Unfortunately there was a catch. He kept tabs on her by denying her any of her own walking-around money. Without cash she was forced to use only his personal credit to run their household. In this way he could be privy to everything she bought, everything she did, everywhere she went and everyone she saw — if curious enough.

Apparently he was curious enough and as he parsed her every act into smaller and smaller pieces, she came to feel trapped in his freakish control. She was miserable from explaining every detail of how she spent every hour, just to ease his incessant distrust. Sometimes he became violent. When she finally prepared herself to leave him, they already had three young children. She was forced to leave them too and, as far as I know, they were never again a part of her life. Betty seldom took guff off anyone and if she had to gnaw off an appendage or two to gain her freedom, then she did.

She eventually landed her Jim Little, still the eligible bachelor, and became my Aunt Bet. They had two babies, my cousins Farley and Seelye, and my family and I would often stay at their rambling estate on Lake Road in Webster, New York. Aunt Bet was a tiny, wiry horse-woman with a gravelly voice who threw her highly kinetic energy into conjuring effortless hospitality.

When we visited, Uncle Jim would tell us, "When the sun touches the water's horizon in just the right way, you might see a green flash!" At cocktail hour the youngsters would be outside on the high bluff overlooking Lake Ontario, hoping to glimpse that elusive burst of color. Behind us the adults clinked their ice cubes in highball glasses,

Cypress Lee, Uncle Jim's house on Lake Ontario

sitting inside the long porch behind a bank of windows that reflected back the setting sun.

Inside, the air was cool and tinged cobalt and aqua where light passed through the nautical glass balls hanging in massive nets set in the room's corners. Sometimes the men would stroll out over the wide lawn, big as a football field, to smack golf balls off the cliff edge beyond us. They'd soar off in wide arcs hitting the water at a distance beyond vision. It was like a being in a postcard depicting the sophistication of an easy life.

When Ann turned 27, she had been at the S&L on Exchange Street in Rochester for over two years. She and the rest of her colleagues were still living in the ill-fitting cocoon of American isolationism, and the European war (which officially began when Germany invaded Poland in 1939) was constantly in the news and on their minds. They all thought, read, talked and argued ad nauseam about whether or not Americans should enter the overseas conflict. The tensions between getting in or staying out shifted back and forth with every new atrocity revealed.

The decision came after the first attack on U.S. soil occurred on a Sunday, December 7, 1941. In the office the following Monday there was little sign of infighting about whether or not we were going to war. The Imperial Japanese warriors had just assaulted us in our own country. They had hit military outposts all over the Pacific, with attacks terrifying in their precision, approximating one target per hour for seven hours, including our base in Hawaii.

As the broadcast news ricocheted around the world, even hardened pacifists seemed to be thrown into an angry delirium. Within a week, some 400 miles south of Rochester, in Washington D.C., President Franklin Delano Roosevelt changed the calculus for everyone as he convened a joint session of Congress. He delivered his famous "day of infamy" speech, finishing with a request for a Declaration of War against Japan. There was only a single dissenting vote in the chamber that day. On Thursday, December 11, Germany and Italy reciprocated by declaring war on the United States.

Ann Little felt her world tilt forward when a telegram addressed to her from the United States Defense Department arrived at the bank. It was the long awaited Civil Service job she had applied for months ago. Her country needed her and she desired nothing more than to get out of Rochester and leave the bank. She ran all the way to her supervisor's office. Rushing in, her lungs pulling for air as she waved the slip of paper in his face, gasping "May I go? May I go?" It was her chance to do something important, change her destiny, to be the somebody she wanted to be.

Taking the job required her to arrive in D.C. at 8:00 AM the next day. With manic energy all was quickly arranged. After some hurried goodbyes, she raced home to Alouette, packed everything she needed, including wet stockings laundered that morning, and impatiently waited for her family. Mama Lit, Bill, Jim and Jane soon rambled up in the old "Tin Lizzie," the late Dr. Lit's treasured motor car, and drove Miss Ann Little to the railroad station. There was just enough time for them to gather around for a last meal before she boarded her train. They were proud of her gumption, and when brother Jim asked "Do you have enough money?" she glibly answered "Oh! Yes, yes of course!" She had $5.00.

Early the following morning she arrived, but while waiting to check her bags, a memory tripped. She had left her stockings hanging from the train's upper berth to dry. Getting them caused a slight delay. Rushing, she then discovered that her destination, "Temporary Bldg. H," was not where she had thought it was, but a mile or two further in. Not an easy sprint, even in her practical moderately low-heeled shoes. Breathless, she ultimately caught up with the other new hires, but only just.

They were a hectic bunch, as equally worried about not being able to find a bed for the night as they were thrilled to find themselves in the nation's capital at such a defining moment. The city was buzzing with adrenaline and filled to capacity with only more people expected. That's when Ann realized she didn't have sleeping accommodations either. Alarmed, she understood $5.00 had never been close to enough.

She had meant to call her friend in town, Jeff Barber, first thing when she got off the train, but that thought had slipped away in the hubbub. When she was given a lunch break, she ran out to locate a phone booth and found she didn't have Jeff's telephone number. Remembering his father was affiliated with the military, Ann decided to track him down instead. In a series of phone calls, eventually leading to the U.S. Navy's personnel office and using only the last name "Barber," no rank, no job description, no home address, she was unbelievably able to make the necessary connection.

It took most of her change and all of her midday break. Worse, Jeff seemed less than pleased to hear from her. Battling the heavy traffic, he picked her up that evening and reluctantly took her back to Union Station, helped collect her luggage and then drove her on to Bethesda, Maryland, where he lived with his parents. Ann was hungry, tired and feeling discombobulated. It was only her first day in town and Jeff Barber looked horrified.

In her memoir, Ann Little describes her arrival at the Barber home:

> I found myself in a rather elegant and formal house. [Jeff's] mother and father [were] very nice but very intellectual and reserved.... It must have been hard on the Barber family to have this crazy girl arrive on their polished doorstep.

Patriotism was running high and there was a palpable urgency to the feeling since links to the "old country" were still strong in our young nation of immigrants. "Uncle Sam Wants YOU" was plastered on every billboard. So the reluctant Barbers did their part in the war effort by allowing my mother to stay in their austere home until she got her first paycheck, an awkward three weeks later. Jeff did his part by finding Ann new accommodations, thereby restoring the genteel peace of his own orderly life. To this end he brought her to the Browns' house on Newark Street in Washington. Ann said pleasantly, "Oh, I know who the Browns are! They are friends of the Franchots, who live on Plymouth Avenue, back home in Rochester. They are our neighbors and dear friends of my parents, so I have heard a great deal about the Browns." She smiled.

In truth, she was thinking it dreadful, since her "dear mother" and Mrs. Franchot had constantly told her what a "great girl" the Brown daughter was. Her name was Caroline and she had been born the day after Ann, on November 5, 1914, for whatever that was worth. She felt sure Caroline was going to be as stuffy as the Franchots, and Caroline was thinking much the same about Ann. It was a suspicious arrangement to them both, compounded by the fact that neither had married (probably for good reasons) and doubly so since their elders had been so pushy in trying to foist this introduction on them since birth.

The $10.00 a week living privileges with the Browns went much better than expected. In the morning, Caroline's father would drop Ann off on his way to work, then each night she would take the crowded, standing room only, streetcar for the hour-long trip back. Her days were grueling in the Office of the Quartermaster General and their employees got only a meager two days off each month, giving her little free time for much else. The glamour of the moment was waning, but luckily, Caroline and Ann had more in common than they first assumed and completely enjoyed each other's company.

Caroline's many friends included some young members of the Swiss Legation. When they were introduced to Ann, her fluent mastery of French generated an instant bond. They knew she was unhappy with her job and, though embassies typically used only their own people, these new friends urged her to apply at their workplace. When a position opened, she applied, got hired and was assigned to the Department of Italian Interests. Ann was feeling très international when she quit her employment with the U.S. government, explaining to her supervisor, "I have to leave because I'm planning to get married." More like a fib than an out and out lie, as she was always planning to get married. She just didn't know when or to whom.

She was quickly aware of her good fortune in being taken on by the Swiss Legation at all. Many of her co-workers could type and take dictation in four different languages and seemingly keep it all straight. Thankfully her initial task at the embassy was simple. She was asked to help fill out renewal applications for Italian passports. It did not go well. When Italian women wed, they keep their maiden name and use their married name as a middle name. After marrying my father, mother's Italian name would have been Ann Tipton Little, the reverse of the American custom. Moreover, if the husband dies, the Italian word for "widow" becomes the middle name, followed by her husband's last name. If mother then became an Italian widow she would be called Ann Vedova Tipton. Her maiden name would drop away altogether.

As Ann sat entering names into forms, a growing list of Vedovas stacked up on her desk. Chatting away with someone across the aisle, Ann happened to mention how many Vedovas there were in Italy, "just like Smiths in the U.S." Her startled officemate said "Mon Dieu! Didn't you know *vedova* means widow?" Mother had misfiled hundreds of immigration packets by placing all widows under V for Vedova. Chagrined, she worked into the wee dark hours untangling the mess she had made before anyone was the wiser.

Ann had to be thrifty and got into the habit of bringing a packed lunch, usually shredded wheat with cream and sugar. Sometimes she would visit Mathilda, an émigré she had helped at work who occupied a tiny space in the Italian Embassy on 16th Street. She was let in by the doorman, Celotto. His family represented the sole Italian staff remaining at the embassy after Pearl Harbor.

Celotto had stayed on to take care of the building, vacant after Mussolini had formed an alliance with Germany in 1936. He considered December 7th, 1941, his "Day of Infamy" too and had been ashamed of his country when he heard President Roosevelt's radio broadcast and call to war. When Ann first met him, he proudly recounted a story of getting off the boat at Ellis Island. According to him, within minutes of landing, he spied two folded 20-dollar bills waiting in a gutter along the streets of New York. He assured her, from that day on, he called himself a "Proud American" and continued to firmly believe in the benevolence of his new country.

Ann enjoyed her lunches in the embassy's quiet courtyard much more than visiting Mathilda inside her claustrophobic living space. Mathilda was paranoid and an avid Jew hater, at first acting insulting and dubious towards my mother, thinking she was Jewish due to her "Livingston Nose." She lived deep in the empty building and Ann had to mount a marble staircase, pass shrouded statues and traverse long echoing corridors to arrive at her door. Mathilda made scathing remarks about everyone she knew and didn't believe anyone over the age of 25 could be a virgin, though a firm Miss Little repeatedly assured her that she was saving herself for "just the right fellow."

In the large institutional bathroom there were a few appliances and an old refrigerator where the two prepared their meals. On one of her visits, Mathilda offered to "share a can of mice." In thickly accented English, she had used the Italian word for corn, or *mais*, which sounds a lot like "mice." Ann reflexively gagged and had to hold herself in check so as not to offend the sour old refugee. She found Mathilda repugnant and creepy on a number of different levels, many of which she never consciously analyzed, but mostly she felt a deep sympathy for the closed off woman and continued to be charitable towards her.

Ann had settled in and truly liked helping people with her work at the Embassy. It was not too close to downtown, but still at the center of all the scuttlebutt floating around about troop movements and their military operations. In addition she had more time for a social life and there were dances at the Sulgrave Club on Dupont Circle and dinner parties given at the Browns' when Rochester friends came to town.

She continued her family's tradition of noblesse oblige with her good works, including various Junior League and church initiatives, but truly enjoyed pitching in at the Traveler's Aide Booth, where she helped smooth the way for newcomers trying to find lodging. She remembered her own poorly planned arrival and found available private homes for sleepy pilgrims of war. Despite her work, her friends and her volunteering for the community, Ann was restless.

One evening, Caroline's sister, Joyce, mentioned that the Red Cross needed women to serve overseas. One had to be over 25, preferably single and of good reputation. Caroline and Ann turned to each other saying "Perfect!" at the same time, and linked pinkies. They were first vetted by the FBI and then accepted into the Red Cross as recruits. There was a 6-week wait period for transportation, during which time they were fitted for uniforms, given some basic training and tasked with a few work assignments to keep them busy until they shipped out. The Red Cross mission was "to prevent or stop human suffering without discrimination."

From Washington, D.C., Ann was sent to Richmond, Virginia, and ultimately to the Merchant Marine Rest Center in Gladstone, New Jersey. This is where regular seamen from all over the world, who had been instrumental to the United States in any military initiative, went to recuperate. These civilian mariners had been torpedoed, kidnapped, tortured or otherwise hurt, providing logistical support for wartime combat forces. The diagnostic term for their illness was "shell shock," which later changed to "combat fatigue," with a range of symptoms considered to be exclusive to military experiences.

Now the syndrome is called Post Traumatic Stress Disorder (PTSD) and applies to any "unimaginable act of

Ann in Red Cross uniform

violence" resulting in very particular effects. Regardless of the original aggression the outcomes are similar. Reliving the event, disassociation from one's self, a lizard-brain sensibility and reflexive anxiety all come together in the ugly package of PTSD. Common triggers for inducing the condition's symptoms include rape, brain injury, catastrophic events, industrial accidents, experiencing abuse as a child, imprisonment and torture.

Ann Little's first job with the Red Cross was situated in a self-contained rehab unit in the center of a large wooded estate. It had been made available as a gift from a wealthy woman whose husband had suffered PTSD during WW1. It had a swimming pool, a functioning dairy, walking trails, tennis courts, riding horses and beautiful gardens providing flowers and vegetables for the ailing men to harvest. Ann found the work redemptive. Her fluent French gave her a skill that made her an asset to many of the internationals, and the setting reminded her of Alouette. There was a nearby lake outfitted with sailboats similar to the ones her brothers used to own and she would often take the former sailors onto the lake in the manageable watercraft. Sometimes she would just swim and float with them, trying to help them regain what they had lost, hoping they could find their way back to the water, back to their life.

No doubt their condition troubled Ann. Seeing these pitiful men must have stirred something inside her, made her wonder at her decision to join the Red Cross and put herself in a danger that could wreak so much devastation on the human body and mind. But maybe not. By our mid-20s, most people have just begun to know their strengths, who they might become or what they cherish. Ann's life, up until that moment, taught her she could change her destiny. She believed in self-determination.

Ann accepted the chance she was taking, it was a worthy dare. Sitting there in a boat next to a shattered man, the very manifestation of vulnerability, it is no wonder that she later described the moment as "very dramatic." Her orders came by way of a disembodied voice megaphoned out across the water. "Will Miss Ann Little please report to the St. George Hotel in Brooklyn, New York, for shipment to overseas post."

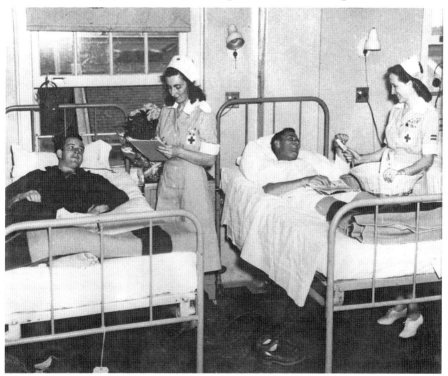

Ann at the New Jersey Merchant Marine Rest Center

PART THREE

THE WAR YEARS

Chapter 17

THE TIDES OF TRANSFER

Ann Little and Caroline Brown were amazed to be reunited when they arrived in New York to await departure for Europe. They had serendipitously been called in from their different work details at the same time. The Red Cross initiates were ordered to come wearing regular street clothes, since troop movements were closely guarded and a mass of uniformed women convening in a public square would certainly be noticed. They had a few days layover, so one evening Ann and Caroline decided to go to the famous Stage Door Canteen in their civilian best.

The nightspot had free admission and was lovingly created for entertaining GIs before they headed off to war. It was a popular place where everyone went to "see and be seen" supporting their American boys fighting overseas. The nightclub had developed a glamorous reputation due to its high-profile clientele and was touted as a spot where "Bette Davis served the desserts, Red Skelton told the jokes, Bing Crosby crooned and stars like Marlene Dietrich and Lauren Bacall danced the night away."

On the way to the club a stranger walked up to Ann and said, "Beware. The spoken word can never be retracted; the unspoken word can never be repeated." She didn't know what that meant, but it put her on edge. When they got to the club, she noticed negro hostesses serving the negro servicemen and thought, "how democratic," but then got flustered out on the dance floor when a black man cut in on the sailor she was dancing with. Ann turned and gamely reached up with open hands, ready for the embrace.

The man was burly and dark. Something about him made her sure he was spoiling to get some kind of reaction out of her, an open demonstration of prejudice or just downright rejection. She was determined not to let any of that happen. A question went through her mind, "Is this the same Ann Livingston Little who recently danced with men where only a formal introduction would do?" After all, wasn't he going to war with the rest of them? And his uniform was crisp with the scent of bright sunshine. It was a novel experience for her, but very quickly a frowning soldier cut in. He was white, of course, and probably ended the potential fracas. Ann felt pride in herself, but also relief and worry all jumbled up. It would be another 20 years before civil rights would be the law of the land and far longer than that before racism, in its many forms, would be fully exposed.

At the New York Port of Embarkation, the entire ARC (American Red Cross) group had to get final shots, attend lectures on security issues, learn about military discipline, as well as master toxin contamination drills. The women were all given personal respirators and briefed on the different types of noxious gases they might be subjected to during their upcoming tour. Next, they were instructed to enter a gas chamber and were then timed on how fast they could put their masks on properly and vacate. They had to repeat the test until they could get it down to within a certain number of seconds. It sent shudders through Ann's body just thinking about why she might need a gas-mask. Some of the women dropped out immediately and returned home.

New ARC workers were equipped with a mess kit (water flask, collapsible cup, utensils and a combination frypan-plate), a musette bag for sundries and a Government Issue pocketbook. Each item had either a shoulder-strap or a pistol-belt so they could navigate hands-free during their travels. There was also a heavy cotton sleeping bag and yellow slicker which they were to pack inside a standard size footlocker.

The women were given a list of all the other necessities they would need to supply for themselves, which included articles of clothing for off-duty leisure time. Expecting to be gone for at least 18 months, Ann wasted the first precious four inches of her trunk by layering the bottom with two years' worth of Kotex. After that came necessary toiletries, 4 pairs of good walking shoes, night clothes, itchy woolen long-johns, a sewing kit, writing materials, bras, slips, and lots and lots of extra panties. Ann made sure there was room for the classic red evening gown/jacket ensemble that sister Jane had picked out for her to take along.

At 8:22 PM the big moment came to embark, the packing and repacking over, as the 180 Red Cross volunteers queued up along Pineapple Street beside the St. George Hotel. They were exhilarated, nervous, scared. They shouted last minute directions to no one in particular, wondered aloud about which ship would be theirs. Hugging and jumping, they tried to calm themselves. Their trunks had been picked up at midnight and were already stowed on board.

Although Ann had followed orders and was appropriately geared up in her winter uniform, with helmet, gas mask and three Government Issue bags slung across her shoulders, many in the group were trying to carry on too many extra parcels. One overladen woman couldn't manage it all. Giving up she begged Ann, "Can you please take this little book? It keeps getting away from me!" as she dropped it once again, trying to rearrange her trappings.

People watching them from their apartment windows, across the street from the "George," began yelling to them, asking "Where are you going? Where are you going?" They couldn't answer, they didn't know. Soon the words grew into a chant that swelled and widened, loudly thrumming the Red Cross girls into the waiting bus and onto the elevated highway; so much for troop security or making a discreet exit. On the ride, they cried out their disappointment as the bus passed by the docked Queen Mary and continued on. She would not be their transport.

When they reached their destination, they were first lined up by twos and then rearranged into single file, still struggling with criss-crossed straps and bulging totes. It was cold and drizzly, and a pair of ARC workers were standing by, ready with comfort food and drink. Some of the frazzled women were trying to accept the offered coffee and doughnuts, but none of them could ignore the hoots coming from the keyed-up soldiers behind them. The men couldn't stop their loud preening for the girls; they were dealing with their own bulky equipment and pounding hearts.

Somewhere a band started playing and none of it seemed real. The young women's alternating emotions were too dynamic to get a sense of it all. Even their feet touching the gangplank seemed to be churning in concrete as they quickly stepped their way up the side of the ship's hull. When Caroline found her room and flung herself on a top berth next to an open window, someone nearby said, "I'm going home!" in a sweet British accent. Hah!! Lying on her bunk, Caroline had the answer. They were all headed to England!

Ann and Caroline and the rest of the over 25-year-old, reputable, husbandless ladies were being herded onto an all-male British troop ship. There was to be no hanky-panky onboard. One of the first things they had all learned during their Red Cross Training was they should be prepared to say "No" a thousand times a day to every sort of sexual overture. This was not a problem for Miss Ann Little – she had set high standards for loosening her iron-clad virtue.

She and three others were assigned to one tiny lower level cabin. It was utilitarian, including only the barest of essentials, being originally intended for the ship's crewmen. The hatch opened into a narrow aisle, featuring a miniscule washbasin at the other end and double berths on either side. They were informed that hot water would only be available from 5:00 to 7:00 PM. The latrine was out and down the gangway a few yards and there was barely enough room for undressing. The beds were exactly as wide as their standard-size trunks, which were in place, labeled with their stenciled first initials and last names facing out.

Caroline had it worse. She was one of 11 women crowded into a space originally built as a stateroom for two, before the luxury liner was requisitioned by the military. It was on the "promenade" deck where upper echelon travelers once took strolls and tea, but was now knee deep in military gear heaped around triple-stack bunks in multiple rows for troops. As the 10-day voyage progressed, the acrid smell of the sleeping men wafting in through the porthole became so concentrated that it was impossible to sleep. Caroline learned to breathe out with her nose, never in.

Two meals were supplied daily at 10:00 AM and 8:30 PM. The British galley served up a questionable fish soup for mid-morning and some other equally unpalatable dish in the evening. There were so many bodies to feed onboard that the chow line seemed to be in constant rotation. Caroline's deck was the starting point for the never-ending food queue, and every day she joined the march around and down, around and down to the mess hall. All the while she was being passed by a long procession of people going back and up, back and up with their plates.

The deck serving meals was piled high with life rafts, which made seating problematic and walking a challenge. During the first daily lifeboat drill there was the rule that no more than two women were allowed per boat. After the foghorn blasted, everyone put on their orange "Mae West" life-vests to race to their places. It was chaos. The women acted like a flock of guinea hens, squabbling around, bumping into each other with squeaks and chattering, getting in the way of sailors trying to lower the rafts and generally ruining any pretense of an orderly escape plan.

The men were no better with their whistles and cat calls, lobbing jokes and lewd comments at the women and generally not taking the exercise seriously. The Captain stopped mid-drill and ordered, "All females back to your living quarters and stay out of the way during all future drills." My mother wasn't surprised.

If you didn't have a job, there wasn't too much to do on a ship. Ann often went top-side during the day and passed the time smoking cigarettes and talking to the enlisted men. At night after supper, everyone gathered in the ship's lounge. She and her buddies staked out the only spot with any elbow room, crouched under the grand piano up on a little stage in the center of things. The whole place was crowded with smoke and jostling people. She noted that most of the gals onboard were more interested in the officers as opposed to the lower ranks. She and Caroline decided the officers had unattractive expectations. Their bloated attitudes and conceited talk usually wound them around to a blatant and predictable come-on line.

On the other hand the lowly foot soldiers were funny and teased like brothers. Ann was often the lone woman in a group of regular GIs ("Government Issues") during much of the trip. The men came from All Over, USA, and were typically young and eager to be there, the momentum of war pulling them along in a headlong frenzy of patriotism mixed with altruism. Others were reservists, activated to fill a void left by someone, just like them, who had already been lost.

Ann, with her brother-in-law Monty (left) and brother Bill, 1943, before going to England to serve in the Red Cross

Ann found herself trying to understand each of them, doing her Red Cross best to lift morale, ease fear. They were Bill or Jim or Monty – all her family now in uniform. It was also flattering to have men giving her their attention. Still unmarried, approaching the end of her 20s, they reminded her that she might still be lovable. Giving them her time kept her mind focused on their needs. The talks felt crucial.

When an enemy plane was spotted and fired on, the alarm went off and all Red Cross Girls were ordered to their cabins. Ann already knew exactly where she stood in the pecking-order of things. If the lifeboat drills were any indication, then the maritime dictum "women and children first" didn't hold true here. They were dispensable. She busied herself by applying her favorite nail polish color, The Toast of New York, by Revlon, thinking "better to go down well groomed," as she considered each of her companions. Which of them would crack, which would be heroic, what would she do if the ship was surrounded? Fired on? Captured? Her mind whirled to every possibility until the activity on deck changed tone. The alert was over, the threat gone and her outward cool made her feel superior as she climbed back up onto the deck, and tried to breathe.

Each night after curfew the ship went into black-out, something they would all get used to, and she and her cabin-mates passed the time lying on their bunks trading gossip and forming friendships. For entertainment they read aloud to one another. The first time an MP knocked on the door after lights-out, they all jumped up in a panic, until he said, "S'cuse me, don't mean to bother, but could you just crack your door a little? I'm having a hard time hearing the story." He was their personal nighttime watchman and had rested his head against the door, overhearing them inside going mutter-mutter-mutter, then Ha Ha Ha, then mutter-mutter-mutter. He couldn't resist knowing what all the fuss was about.

The girls had been sharing the little book that had been thrust on Ann at the loading platform. It was an engaging story called *A Tree Grows in Brooklyn,* by Betty Smith. It's about an Irish immigrant family surviving in New York during the early 1900s and is one of many such books American publishers distributed to troops in WW2. It was produced in a special portable format called The Armed Service's Editions and fit nicely into a military uniform pocket.

This is a transcript of a PBS radio interview with author Guptill Manning speaking about a wounded soldier who had written to the author of the book, Betty Smith:

> He [the soldier] asked a nurse for a book because he was bored and had nothing else to do. She happened to give him a copy of *A Tree Grows in Brooklyn,* and the book just changed his entire outlook. It made him laugh, it made him cry. And he said even though a battle-hardened Marine usually doesn't cry, he was proud of his tears because it proved that he was human again.

The WW2 books-for-soldiers initiative was more than just a kindness to the overseas ranks, it helped launch *The Great Gatsby* and many other publications into the 20th-century reading mainstream. My mother never again saw the woman who had entrusted her with that little book, but she considered it a godsend at the time. Ann Little would always keep a copy of Betty Smith's book on hand. It stood as a reminder of the tight quarters on the troop ship and of her interactions with the young soldiers and hopeful Red Cross Girls, the majority of whom were away from home for the first time.

When Ann, Caroline and the rest of the women disembarked in Scotland, Ann was charmed to be welcomed by tartan-kilted men, many with red beards, playing the festive sounds of traditional Celtic music on reedy bag-pipes. Best of all were the two American Red Cross sisters who greeted her with fresh coffee and doughnuts. She hadn't realized it was so late, the breakfast meal of fish soup was long gone and the day had somehow rolled on into late afternoon. What a warm reception.

Troops from America had been landing there for the past two years and up until that moment Ann had mistakenly supposed the locals would be disgusted with yet another boatload of Yanks crowding onto their island. As she and her bevy of women boarded a train to London, they had no idea of what to expect next.

Chapter 18

WHAT WORKS EXCLUDES WHAT DOESN'T

Personal correspondence was secured by the government in a special way during WW2. Letters were photographed, censored, and then processed onto microfilm in large batches called "Victory Mail," which were then flown back to the States and distributed using the regular postal service at home. In Ann's first "V Mail," dated October 11, 1943, she describes to her mother her train ride through Scotland:

> As we rode through the beautiful countryside, children came running to wave at us. A woman picking flowers in her garden waved her bouquet at me. A man with his chin covered by a foamy white lather waved his shaving brush out the window. As we sped through the night, we stopped at intervals for more food and hot drinks. Our compartment contained about eleven beautiful girls (eleven) smoking and playing Black Jack by the light of one tiny blue bulb — with our hats on the backs of our heads and tossing cigarette butts into an upturned tin helmet — we must have looked as though we were plotting some crime.

At the American Red Cross headquarters in London, Ann and Caroline were asked to choose which aspect of troop support suited their abilities. Ann could speak French, but France had not yet opted into the fray. Of the available options, she knew she was best suited to be a hostess, thinking of her summer days at Alouette, where she and her family made their own fun by playing parlor games like charades and throwing impromptu dinner parties for the whole neighborhood. The two friends hoped they would be stationed where they could do the most good, but they also hoped they could be kept together as a team. It was a hot topic for them and there was much discussion over where they might get posted and why.

In a 1943 letter to Aunt Topsy, Ann wrote about her work options in the ARC:

> It seems a soldier can be in three places – in camp – in the hospital – or on furlough – but there is also a fourth place and that is where his thoughts are...home. So the ARC has those four services all linked together: Club Service, Camp Service, Hospital

Service, and Home Service. I am [hoping to be] in the Club Service and will be situated in some metropolitan or central area where the men may come in to enjoy their free time.

Major sources for this book: Ann's 1944 diary with her journal "A Red Cross Gal on the Move" tucked inside, along with v-mails (lower left), letters on Red Cross letterhead, and Jim's hand-written memoir and U.S.A.F. Oral History

They were required to pick from one of three Club divisions, Navy Fleet Clubs, Army Camp Clubs or Air Corp Aero Clubs; they both chose Aero Clubs. At the time, there was little ground fighting; the sky was where the action was. One questionnaire seemed designed to find any unusual qualifications or "special talent" they might have. The two friends assumed it would be used for placement purposes, and were hoping their similar backgrounds would keep them together. But no — the system involved two columns, one for names, one for places, both in alphabetical order, side by side. Caroline **B.** went to **B**ovington, Racheal **H.** went to **H**omer, and Ann **L.** went to **M**embury (apparently there were no Aero Clubs beginning with an "**L**"), and that's how it went— right down the line. So much for special talents! She and Caroline were split apart and sent off on separate adventures.

Ann was assigned to Royal Air Force (RAF) Membury, a British airfield built in 1942 and shared by the USA. It had developed into a major supply and maintenance depot and was located about 60 miles west-southwest of London. After several eye-opening days in the capital, Ann boarded a train from Paddington Station to take her new job.

On the train in blackout conditions with no conductors, a traveler had to already know where to get out. Every car had its own doors opening to the outside, and Ann was the only passenger left in her compartment when it was time to get off. She furiously hoped she had counted the correct number of stops as she stepped down, directly onto a metal track, the air dark as pitch, while the train began to pull off and away. As her eyes adjusted, she was relieved to find herself just a short trek from the station's platform and even more relieved when she dimly perceived someone in the shadowy darkness, hopefully waiting for her. She could barely make him out, under an unearthly blue light.

Soon after settling into her new post, Ann wrote to Jane about exploring London before getting to Membury in a letter dated October 14, 1943:

> I spent a few days there. The night life is something. Four ARC gals started out of a Monday evening. We were looking for one of the service clubs to which Judy, one of the four, had been assigned. In our search in the blackout we spied a café. Not being sure whether or not it was proper for us to enter unescorted, we asked a Bobby [policeman] what he thought about the situation. He said it was quite alright. So we found ourselves standing in the foyer feeling a little uncertain. With that, two flyers came up and said they would take us in. WELL it turned out to be the headquarters of the Piccadilly Commandos. Prostitutes to you! It seems the place is famous throughout the world. I wish you could have seen the glances we received as we sat there in a prim little row against the wall, sipping our brandy in silence. We, in turn, stared at them. Fat, highly rouged, dyed blonds – one of them even sported a red wig! The boys just shrugged their shoulders at us and smiled. As Jim says, "You can't hop on one foot," so we had another drink and went on our way, feeling that we had seen "Life."
>
> The next night Caroline and I went out freelancing. First to the Carleton, then to the Dorchester, there we were again picked up by two flyers, we ditched one at the Stork Club and I took on

three more. Two of them left my group at yet another hot spot and I returned home at an early hour with someone called Bud. Bud it seems was lonely. He had been here for thirteen months and had no relations with P.C.s [prostitutes] and he was SO GLAD to see an American girl – Ah me! I was SO GLAD to see my seven beautiful roommates (seven) when the evening drew to a close and I was STILL INTACT!

Guess I won't try London again for quite a while. Not until the next time anyway. My new post has me stumped. As far as I can see the activities are all on the formal, planned, efficient side. In other words no spontaneous fun – perhaps when I know the lay of the land I'll enjoy my assignment more. Please write. Love from Ann.

The two other ARC workers at the Membury Club were both named Marion, so the enlisted men had dubbed them Mark1 and Mark2, like two iterations of the same weaponry. All the overseas Red Cross women were given the rank of Captain, in case of capture, hoping their higher grade would give them better treatment if taken prisoner. Being officers also allowed them the option of taking meals with the higher ups, instead of the enlisted men.

The title produced the not-too-subtle effect of reinforcing a bias favoring officers on "first dibs" for the girls. Mark1 had this all figured out. She worked the system hard. She would loll in bed till noon issuing orders over the telephone – lining up supplies, entertainment, transportation and anything else she could make use of – and then spent the rest of her time "primping for effect" before leaving her room to turn some heads at the officer's mess.

At night Mark1 would sometimes tag along with a couple of rowdy Texan officers on clandestine hunts. They'd take the company jeep out into the dark countryside in all-wheel drive, one steering, the other riding the fender with his handgun out, ready to pick off rabbits caught stilled in the headlights. These two cowboys were permitted access to the grounds of Rook's Nest, a nearby landed estate owned by a widow named Mrs. Spotteswood, in return for alcohol. Mrs. Spotteswood was partial to gin, and Mark1 made sure she found plenty of that particular joy. When the poachers had enough fresh meat, an uncommon wartime delicacy, they'd carry it into the canteen's kitchen and create a big feast, a special bounty to offer the ARC women for joining them in their improvised dining room.

Ann felt very uncomfortable with Mark1's Rook's Nest setup. Their mission was to create a wholesome oasis for soldiers away from home and bribing the widow for sport hunting was unseemly. Besides it was inconsiderate to the local farmers who relied on small game for food. She didn't argue; she was new and uniquely compromised. Not only were the suppers a welcome diversion, but more importantly she wanted to keep being invited to late afternoon tea by Mrs. Spotteswood. Ever since Ann had arrived in England, the weather had been bitter. She hated scratchy wool, but wore her long-johns anyway, just to keep her teeth from shivering inside her head.

The only time Ann felt warmth without itch was when she was inside the widow's enormous fireplace. It was so big it was reputed to have a hidden staircase running up the chimney, a place where Catholics hid during Britain's Reformation in the 1500s. Two sitting-alcoves were cut into each corner behind the big hearth. Tucked inside, Ann could feel the surrounding stones radiating their heat deep into her core. It was also an unusual vantage point. Looking out through the flames Ann watched the other guests glow and flicker back at her, darkly framed by the room behind them. These pleasures would be hard to give up.

When Mark1 left and Mark2 became Club Director, Ann became the assistant director. By then she was dedicated to catering to the enlisted men. Her female colleagues still fell all over themselves trying to get noticed by the commanders, but she was way beyond that. She preferred the attention she got from the rank and file; they were mostly men that would be going back to civilian jobs when the war was over, and that suited her. They were easier to handle than the self-important officers and she didn't feel as judged by them. She wanted to be noticed for who she was, what she did. After all, this was no dog and pony rodeo.

She learned that G.I. Joes had three major areas of complaint. She got it. She got it when they griped about the officers (their bosses), the Red Cross Girls (officer's bait) and every country they occupied (not home). She got it and felt compassion for them and their frustrations, frustrations as familiar as her own. She made her footlocker into a coffee table by throwing a square of burlap over it. She was glad to give the boys a place where they could be themselves, give voice to their perplexities.

Everyone knew that gambling and alcohol were strictly prohibited at ARC canteens, but bingo and smoking were fine. These were the rules and Ann always tried to play by the rules. The club regularly held dances every Saturday night, inviting girls in the Women's Land Army from the neighboring farms to attend. Many of them had relocated from urban areas, offering their labor to help feed the country. Everyone in England was doing their bit and these girls were doing theirs by serving as replacements for the men who usually worked the farms but were away being warriors.

Mark 2 and Ann had been training the new recruit, Jeannie Karaganis, who just had transferred in. Their first Saturday dance working together happened to land on October 30th, the night before All Hallows Eve. It was late afternoon and they had been preparing for the event all day when 35 barrels labeled Sweet Apple Cider were delivered to the canteen. It came in a shipment that had been previously ordered by Mark1, shortly before she left. When Ann tasted it she wasn't sure if it was alcoholic or not. She asked Jeannie to taste it and Jeannie thought it seemed alright. Besides, it was delicious and much better than what they had on hand. Its arrival truly seemed like providence, an unexpected holiday treat. They went with it.

Mark 2, Ann and Jeannie had transformed their office into a House of Horrors by stringing up army blankets on rafters to create a maze. They placed slimy spaghetti-worms on tables for hands to find as they groped their way forward in the dark woolen tunnel. They hung limp gauze at face level, creating the illusion of brushing into spider webs. They found someone who could moan in unearthly tones and scream like a demon. They enlisted a volunteer goblin to jump out, flashlight under chin, to jolt the maze walkers into a bloody terror just as they exited the back door, hopefully laughing as they hit the cold night air.

To foster a little innocent titillation Ann had the idea for an adult variant on a favorite Halloween game. She dangled apples midair on strings. The object was for one of the GIs to pick a farm girl and bob at the fruit between them, hands behind their backs, using only their teeth. The tempting fresh apples doubled as a pretty decoration.

Ann had also stitched together real witches' costumes, complete with black pointy hats. To heighten the effect, all three slathered lipstick around their eyes and blacked out each other's teeth with wax pencils. After the transformation, they couldn't stop looking at each other, laughing when they cackled like storybook crones. Ann was wicked scary with her long Livingston Nose. They felt quite ready for their unsuspecting guests.

The women showed up first. Mark2 was stationed at the maze, Ann was responsible for serving the refreshments, and Jeannie was a floater to keep a chaperone-eye on the floor. Next the men strolled in, ignoring the three ugly witches. Looking around, they plucked the apples right out of the air, as if from a tree, chomping down as they grinned at their potential partners. The female tenant workers looked sweet with their chapped legs glowing red under their gathered party-skirts, straining to begin the dance. For their part, the boys were eyeing the warm dark maze as a prospective lover's lane, hoping for a little squeeze in the dark.

The mixer was an exuberant success. Even though the apple bobbing idea was a flop, the boys showed no sign of being awkward and readily mingled with the girls. Some of them formed tight groups huddled around tables chatting and listening to the band, while others jumped in and started showing off their latest jitterbug moves, twirling the girls so their skirts flew out behind them. Others coupled off and got in line for the maze, eager to make their way slowly through the blankets. Inside, the girls predictably screamed and many jumped into the arms of their would-be protectors. A few pairs didn't find their way out for a long, long time. Everyone seemed to be in high spirits.

Ann secretly considered the event to be her private celebration; she would turn 29 in just five days and Halloween had always been a favorite holiday. She had arrived only a few weeks ago and she was already next in line to be an ARC director. If she got the chance, she would set a higher standard for her hospitality club than Mark1 had. Things would still be done properly, just with a little more flare. This party was a perfect example of how slight innovations could make things more exciting. The dance was getting louder and presently Jeannie found Ann at her station dispensing drinks and asked "Do you think the cider's got a kick?" just as the first fist-fight broke out on the dance floor and total havoc ensued.

Mark2 came rushing over and Ann immediately stopped serving the cider. The witches were fairly ineffective as they swooped into action, flapping like three cawing crows. They were trying to get control of a situation that had already gone out of bounds. It took a good long while to clear out the tipsy revelers, especially from the maze, which seemed to have grown more nooks and crannies. Ann suspected that some of the more sophisticated in the bunch might have sipped a cocktail or two before coming to the dance, but the teetotalers probably didn't know what hit them. At any rate there were a lot of inebriated folks losing their inhibitions by letting fly all sorts of pent-up energy.

Late into the night an M.P. had to throw one soldier into the brig. He was caught with one foot in and one foot out of Mark2's office window. He pitifully said he was just trying to get more of that wonderful apple stuff. Unfortunately he got court-martialed and was ordered to clean the sticky floors of the club, which he did, directing hard looks at the Red Cross staff as he pushed the mop around.

Feeling guilty, Ann tried to explain to their supervisor that it was her fault the young man got into trouble. She was the one serving intoxicating beverages that didn't taste like booze. The chief of operations said that would just constitute another criminal charge.

Mark2 quickly sold the remaining kegs to another outfit, and then their delivery truck ran into a ditch during transport. The entire event was bad news all around. Ann should have known, she felt horrible remorse and figured Mark1 knew very well that was hard cider when she ordered it. The joke was on her.

Chapter 19

INTO THE FRYING PAN

It was with some relief to Ann when the Photo Reconnaissance Group moved out and the 366th Fighter Group moved in two months later. The canteen learning curve had been steep and she was eager to make a better impression on the new boss, Colonel Meyer. As part of the advance team, the deputy, a Lt. Colonel J.B. Tipton, showed up at Membury RAF base where Ann and Jeannie were throwing a Christmas Eve party. Since it was being held at the Officers Club, everyone was drinking. Ann had remembered the trick of writing letters on the ceiling with the soot of burning candles and they were making a game of it, laughing like little children, heads thrown back, arms high in the air writing messages in smoke when he walked in. She was wearing her red evening gown.

When Jim Tipton saw Ann Little, he could not have had a neutral response. She looked like his wife back in Texas. He must have been instantly attracted to her, as well as repelled. He found the situation somewhat disgraceful, seeing American females – these "camp followers" – all dressed up, cavorting around overseas with a bunch of soldiers instead of staying put, stateside and safe where they belonged. He figured they were up to no good. He got a drink, put it on the fireplace mantle, turned and hoisted himself up to perch next to his cocktail. It was a graceful, powerfully athletic move for such a tall man, and Ann noticed. She thought he was a showoff. That would be typical for an officer.

Jim talks about his first two weeks on the ground as a newly minted deputy and Lt. Colonel in his USAF "Oral History." His description of meeting Ann Little is reminiscent of the way he handled Ann Weaver in this 1985 interview—not accurately in the case of the former, and not at all in the case of the latter. This is his "official" version of that initial encounter with my mother (p. 21):

> I met my [second] wife on Christmas Eve of 1943. I had been in England less than a week. I got to my new airbase as advance party for the 366th Fighter Group; that's how I got into war. I was the advance party in England. My wife was a Red Cross Girl there; there were two of them. I met her and I didn't even remember her, really, except they were having a Christmas Eve

party at the club. I just pulled out of an airplane up in Prestwick and had got out to the airbase at Membury. I met the girl right then and there, having no idea in the world I would ever see her again. It wasn't love at first sight at all.

Here is the V-mail Ann sent to Jane and Monty on December 26, 1943, two days after that first exchange with the Lt. Colonel — whom she doesn't mention at all:

> Christmas went off pretty well. The very first present I opened was to Aunt Ann with love from Nicky and Johnny and of course I started to cry. Having a little eggnog fixed that up temporarily. One of the boys brought me a dozen eggs [and] I purchased the bottle [of alcohol] at 2 pounds, 15 shillings through the efforts of an electrician friend. We went pub crawling one night and he found a man who knew where, etc. etc.

The electrician was named Mike and he did various jobs around the base, including collecting Red Cross Girls from the train station. He was an NCO (non-commissioned officer), so he had come up through the enlisted ranks and was older and more mature than the typical GI. In Ann's first week in Membury he came by to fix a wiring problem in her quarters and they had gotten into deep conversation while he worked on it. His eyes held a perpetual smile, just at the corners. He came around the next day, supposedly to retrieve a pair of pliers. They talked again.

She enjoyed his wry humor. He was solicitous towards her, and she didn't discourage him. He kept finding reasons to drop by, often by coming back for a little something he had left behind, checking on an electrical gadget or fixing some tripped connection. She began to look for him wherever she went. When Ann thought about him, her face rearranged itself into a lopsided grin. When they left each other's company she felt compelled to turn around to watch him as he walked away. He was irresistible and he knew it.

Here is the rest of Ann's December 26, 1943, V-mail:

> After opening all my presents Marion [Mark2] and I went over for a large turkey dinner, complete with cranberry sauce, then I took a lot of cigarettes over to the hospital and talked to the boys there for a while. By that time it was the hour to get cracking on our "open house." Our cook had been baking for weeks and we held the doors open for all and sundry. Even the officers were invited. We had mince pie, fruit cake, fruit salad, sliced meat,

potato salad and mountains of cookies. All the lights were out except for the Christmas tree and candles on the tables.... The boys were quite subdued.

The cute things they say make it all very worthwhile.... One boy came to wish me a "Merry Christmas" after carol singing (which I led, ha ha) and said he loved me with a purple passion. A little while later he came back and said that he didn't want to spoil the pretty speech he had made by saying another word, but could he please have a ping pong ball?

Ann had always loved group singalongs, ever since her days at Camp Nobscussett. She was enthusiastic, and though she knew her voice was only so-so at best, still she didn't hold back. She knew all the latest songs as well as many old favorites and used her innate ability to remember most of the lyrics to keep the singers moving along. She also taught a French class on weekdays at 9:00 in the morning, visited soldiers in hospital once a week, regularly invited the base Chaplain over to play cards with the men and arranged to bring local children into the Aero Club for seasonal holidays.

Here are excerpts from a letter Ann wrote to Jane, dated January 6, 1944:

I gave a children's party myself this year — three hundred and fifty small moppets arrived at about 2:30 in the afternoon.... They were quite thrilled by it, not having seen such a performance in four years. After that, they went by groups of one hundred into our canteen where the boys showed them to hot chocolate, brioche, fruitcake, cookies, jelly tarts and mountains of candy. We had a tree with presents under it for all and they went home feeling happy.

My job is going along very smoothly now. There are times when it requires much endurance, tact, patience and a lot of other things I do not have an overabundance of, and then there are times when all's right with the world. That is how it is now. My club is pretty and attractive and the men enjoy it to the utmost. I live in a nice warm house and can take a bath every day if I feel like it.

She had been brought overseas to create this toolbox of distractions for the servicemen, but in many ways she felt more like she had been hired on as their den mother. She was worldlier than most of those she served

Children's Christmas party hosted by the American Red Cross,
Membury, England, December 23, 1943

and purposely kept her private affairs separate from the canteen. Her
efforts there were rewarding and she was enjoying her work, but living
it day by day could wear anyone down. Sometimes she had to switch it
up.

Here's an entry in her diary from early 1944:

> January 3: This morning I started forth to learn how to drive a
> 2-1/2 ton truck! After about an hour in the carpark, practicing
> changing gears up and down the scale, I drove right over London
> Bridge, Trafalgar Square, Piccadilly, etc etc!! From ping pong to
> truck driving just like that. Fooled around a little more and re-
> turned to Batts about 5. Mike called for me and we had supper
> at Manettes – not so good this time – he went off to Scotland.

Red Cross workers got a day and a half off every week and there was a
place in London called The Batts where they could stay for free. Blackout conditions made it hard to get around. You could hold your hand in
front of your eyes and not see it, touching your face just to make sure.
On her off days Ann learned to get where she was going by early evening. In London the pubs closed when the buses stopped for the night,

so if you wanted a drink after 10:00 PM, you had to join a "bottle club." These were after-hours spots, somewhat reminiscent of the speakeasies Jane Little had frequented during Prohibition. Ann was glad to have somewhere to go and she never wanted to get stuck out there in the dark by herself.

When out too late, she and her group club-crawled to an obscure American bar that was hard to find and off a narrow side street. They would stay till the sky began to lighten. This is where they picked up the latest rumors, songs and slang. "Boy, you've had it!" was being bandied around constantly. It made no sense, yet it did. Everyone used the phrase all the time for everything. "I'm being reassigned," "My boyfriend gave me a ring," "The fish'n'chips are good here," were all met with, "Oh boy, you've had it now," and it always worked. It was vaguely ironic and seemed to fit every situation.

After Mike took off for Scotland, Ann drove the truck 160 miles to Caroline's Club in Hemel Hempstead, then went on for another 60 miles to visit two other ARC girls staying at The Batts. One, Ruth Ferguson, was a friend Ann had made on the troop ship coming over.

> January 4: [Our group] had dinner at the Maison Basque – after 4 double scotches, we all retired feeling very Irished. At 3:00 AM came the guns and Ruth was down in our room in nothing flat. She turned her ankle on the way down. We sat by the fire and talked about everything. Ruth was in her Aero Club when it got blown to pieces about a month ago and the reaction is just setting in. I never felt anyone shake so. She claims she will get over it in time. Passed my truck driving test today – drove steadily and carefully.

Chapter 20

JUGS AND JOBS AND EUROPEAN HIGH JINX

If Lt. Colonel J. B. Tipton was vexed with Ann Little when he first arrived at the Membury Christmas Party, his boss, Colonel Dyke Meyer, didn't help matters. He insisted that Mark2, Ann and Jeannie should take all their meals at the head table with the senior officers. In his opinion the ARC hostesses were there for his enjoyment. Jeannie preferred eating in the officers' mess hall anyway and was very attentive towards Lt. Colonel Jim Tipton. That was fine with him. Besides, Ann Little ignored him and he wasn't much interested in Mark2.

Once Lt. Colonel Tipton used language around the breakfast table that may have been common vernacular below the Mason-Dixon Line, but it grated on Ann Tipton's more urbane sensibilities. He used a phrase that involved the "N" word to describe a plumbing issue on base. He was talking to his boss, Dyke, in a confidential scoff that the women probably weren't supposed to hear. But Ann did. Not only was the deputy a show off, but he could be a coarse man as well. She wondered at Jeannie's taste in men.

In actuality Jim wasn't paying much attention to the niceties of social interchange. He had plenty of other things on his mind those first few months in the ETO (European Theater of Operations). The suppliers at RAF Membury were outfitting his group's aircraft with "legs" or

Lt. Colonel Jim Tipton with his first "Diablo," a Thunderbolt P-47

extra gas tanks, so the planes could go deeper inland and work tactical interdiction, thereby setting the stage for things to come.

Jim Tipton talks about flying the P-47 Thunderbolts and being with the 366th in his 1985 USAF "Oral History" (p. 26-30):

I don't know how many hours I got, but I didn't get many hours in that jug, the P-47; about 3 or 4 hours checkout as I recall.... It was a sort of big, heavy fighter. It was theoretically designed to be a high altitude fighter, but it turned out to be the greatest fighter bomber you ever saw because it could be shot to pieces and still get home and did — frequently....

Air-cooled engine, but it was a heavy lumbering thing. When I got with the P-51s, of course, that was my basic love, but I was in the P-47 outfit and started my combat with doggoned little training in it. I was deputy commander. What does that mean? I don't know, still don't know. You do whatever you can to protect the boss, that's what you do.

Later on in Europe we [he and Colonel Meyer] flew quite a few missions together. I would lead one mission and he would lead another, so we alternated. When we became combat operational, about February or March, we were doing a lot of escort work. Once in a while we would go over the [English] Channel and work on the ground doing targets of opportunity: hitting marshalling yards, communications, and things like that. Of course we didn't have any close-support work at the time because we didn't have any ground forces on the continent.... As far as we were concerned, we had no contacts at all over there until Normandy came along. The ground attacks that we did were to try to interrupt whatever we could in the way of the war effort.... In any case, Dyke would lead the group on missions, and I would fly his element, which would be No. 3 man in his flight.

In his 1982 memoir, the Lt. Colonel talks about one of his missions from Membury:

Dyke Meyer, the 366th CO was a relatively senior officer for those days and ran a tight ship.... I was the next senior man in the group. However I was also the newest "recruit" in the outfit, the only one who hadn't been through tactical training, and had very few hours in the P-47 Thunderbolt by the time we went operational in England. The one combat mission which returns to my mind is my first dog fight, or should I say Dyke's dogfight.... Although the 366th was assigned to the 9th Air Force, designed for tactical operations, initially we flew full group missions, sweeping the continent.... When Dyke led the group, I often went along as his element leader. And it was so this particular day when we found Jerry [the Nazis], or maybe when he found us. Dyke was a tiger! Full throttle, his fist clenched around his radio button, unaware that he was filling our frequency with his excited remarks about what he was going to do with those S.O.B.s.

His wingman immediately disappeared back in the pack when we accelerated into battle and I thought we had lost him. Excitement, ignorance, inexperience and stupidity on my part, no doubt, but the facts remain; I elected to take over the wing slot and squandered an opportunity esteemed beyond price. I chased after Dyke, dragging my wingman behind me, keeping my head on a swivel, presumed to protect his tail from the attacking Hun who never showed. Indeed, I looked around so conscientiously that Dyke became quite provoked when I couldn't confirm his second aircraft destroyed. There were plenty of F.W.s and 109s [Focke-Wulf and other German aircraft] milling around, but none entered my sight pattern. I never fired a shot.

While Jim Tipton was in the air, Ann Little was on the ground and getting a promotion. On January 17th, 1944, Ann took over as director of the Red Cross unit assigned to RAF Membury. She then proceeded to get into trouble with everybody. First off, the canteen cook, Mrs. Hatchet, came in to report that one of her crew was about to quit because a specific GI came into her kitchen using derogatory language. Ann was aware of the offender and considered him a knuckleheaded bigot. She decided he was probably not a real threat, just a weak scared bully. When she went to confront him, he was asleep in a chair, snoring, and she thought better of it and decided to just leave it alone, let the incident fade away.

That night the ARC closed the canteen in order to host the 16th Air Depot Group's private party. It was her first big event as the new director and when it was over she considered it a failure. Nobody danced with her or commented on the amenities she had spent all day pulling together. To make matters worse, her regulars were incensed that the place had been made off-limits to them.

At breakfast in the officers' mess the next day she was grousing about the thankless night she had endured and stupidly mentioned Mrs.

Hatchet's complaint of foul language directed towards her staff. One of the brass at the table overheard her and insisted on knowing who was cussing out workers in the canteen. Ann reluctantly gave up his name, but only on the assurance it would go no further. He told her it would not. Thinking it over in the middle of the night, she got worried.

First thing in the morning, Ann made a formal call to the rude boy's Commanding Officer to confirm that there should be no repercussions. She ended the conversation with, "after all, he's just a kid." The soldier's CO seemed very understanding of everything she had said, which made her feel fine, until one of the kitchen staff popped into her office complaining, "Hey, what's the big idea of ARC gals getting soldiers court-martialed for swearing?"

That afternoon she passed one of the GIs coming out of her club and he saluted her, saying "You deserve it!" She wasn't sure if he was being sarcastic or not. Later she heard the CO had meted out company punishment, despite his word not to. So much for sidestepping the chain of command; she should have dealt with that young man herself. She'd have to grow thicker skin if she was going to be a director.

The incident ultimately resulted in a formal inspection of the ARC Aero Club. It was during regular working hours and an obvious show of force to the troops milling about the canteen. Miss Little was in trouble. Here is the entry in Ann's diary that details the rebuke:

> January 22: The Red Cross was inspected by the Colonel (Meyer) fourteen hundred two zero hours. Present were a Lt. Colonel, two Majors and two Capts. who all evidenced great interest. They inspected the electric lights even. After a cup of coffee all around, the Colonel patted me on the shoulder and said, "Very nice Ann." In the evening we had the usual Bingo game.

And that was that. Order had been restored. The official use of condescension towards her was bad enough, but it was nothing more than a self-imposed humiliation when it came her turn to bestow a kiss on the big winner of the Bingo game that night. Instead of a regular GI, the recipient was to be the sooty little man who serviced the nineteen pot-bellied stoves that kept the canteen warm.

Everyone knew a "kiss" from one of the Red Cross Girls was always the last prize of the night. But the jeering men were oddly riled up that evening. Jeannie watched in amusement as the little gnome shuffled over and puckered up for the new director. The men hollered boisterous encouragement. They were laughing like they had set the whole thing up, so Ann agreeably mugged for them. She deserved it.

On March 1, 1944, Colonel Adrial "Doc" Williams and his 436th Troop Carrier Group moved into Membury and Colonel Dyke Meyer and his 366th Thunderbolt Group moved 80 miles east to Thruxton. The fighters were going operational and needed to be closer to the action. It was obvious by then that Jeannie had fallen for the deputy and Ann was being overwhelmed by the sergeant. While Lt. Colonel Tipton was busy flying P-47s and taking pot-shots from the ground at V-1 buzz bombs in Thruxton, Miss Little was still serving the GIs in Membury.

The move from Membury to Thruxton forced an unusual alliance between an officer and an enlisted man. Jim Tipton and Mike Regond of the 366th were deeply involved with the two Red Cross girls, Jeannie and Ann. It was a practical arrangement for the men to travel together when they visited their gals. Though fraternizing between the upper and lower echelons was discouraged in the military, it did sometimes happen. They both knew the score and relied on each other's mutual discretion. All is fair in love and war. Amen.

Here are the more revealing entries in Ann's diary regarding E.M.R., a.k.a. Sergeant E. Michael Regond, her electrician friend Mike, after the 366th relocation:

March 8: Mike showed up for the dance. Everything went off OK. Music, food, girls.

March 10: Retired early only to be dragged out by one E.M.R. In the morning we were awakened by [the] Tannoys blaring forth with music from Germany – The little man said it's zero zero hours. That's reveille in the army, boy.

March 13: [The call] to Flemings Hotel for reservations on Thurs and Fri has to be done over again for next Tues and Wed because one of the boys in Mike's outfit swiped the Chaplain's wine and sold it for a fabulous price. Now they are all restricted!!

March 16: I worked like mad all day and stayed up until all hours with Mike talking and talking and talking.

March 21: Then we [Ann and Jeannie] went back to Flemings and met the boys [Mike and Jim]. Several more drinks, dinner and to bed. Only I got up again to watch an air-raid first hand. I started to shake with the cold (or something) upon realizing that someone somewhere in London was getting it. When a flare dropped in the street outside my window I made haste to pop into bed and put the comforter over my head while awaiting the fatal bomb – but it seems I fell asleep.

March 22: Mike and I had a long conversation over a brandy – I was left more confused than ever.

March 23: After Mike left today JBL and I had a talk... [JBL is James Bellows Little, Ann's oldest brother, who was in the RAF. They spoke long-distance.]. All he wants to be sure of is that I do the right thing and that I find happiness. Selfishly though, that's just what I want. With all my doubts on the subject, it would appear that [someone] was correct in this adage – tis better to be unhappily unwed than be unhappily wed – on the other hand, how can one know until one tries? So it seems that in the multitude of soldiers this soul is more alone than ever.

March 31: Jeannie went to Thruxton to a dance while I went pub crawling with Mike and Tom. Played darts and had a lovely time.

April 1: Mike and I drove there [Thruxton] via Swindon and we went through some beautiful country. One place went through a forest of trees with huge gnarled trunks hundreds of years old. Savernake Forest it's called. There was no underbrush, so it seemed almost like being inside a huge gothic cathedral – at the camp I saw a 14' hole that a P-47 pilot dug for himself as a grave.

April 3: Mike called from Membury to ask me to fetch him tootsweet. He seemed to think that he is to get mobile – so in I drove in the rain, picking up paratroopers en route. In the evening we saw Casablanca – a very good movie. We had supper then and played records. How sweet you are seemed to be the theme song.

April 9: E.M.R., Jeannie and I went to church today, after which Jeannie had dinner at the Officers Club, Mike at ARC Aero club and I at General Sir Godley's.

April 15: The usual dance at the Officers Club. I endeavored to obtain a small amount of booze from Lt. Mooring so that I could leave Mike well supplied in case he wished to drown his sorrows while I waltzed with some handsome 2nd Lt. However, when I found that Lt. M. almost had me on my knees begging for the stuff, I suddenly realized that things were going a bit far. So, gathering together what pride I had left, I swished out of the place. Ah me – these G.D.B.F.s of officers. You should have heard me swear!!

April 16: On this day Tom, Jeannie and I drove one E.M.R. back to Thruxton. We ran into Colonel Meyer, Tipton, etc. Nothing to do but we should stay and see a big review. Me, my dress itched and I wanted nothing more than to get out of the place. So Jeannie stayed and watched the award of the D.F.C. [Distinguished Flying Cross]. Sat next to Gen. Quesada, etc. etc. I guess I really missed it.

April 17: Jeannie's birthday. Her Lt. Colonel friend came to see her and brought one E.M.R. with him. While Jeannie went tripping, Mike and I sat about playing records etc. ...Unfortunately I got sleepy and simply had to pop into bed – much to the disgust of el Colonel, to say nothing of el Sergeant – he is a lamb.

April 21: Saturday evening Lt. Colonel Tipton's chauffer Wallbridge called for Jeannie and me at six to take us to Thruxton. I wound up with Major Smith...telling him all my woes. In fact we spent the whole night in conversation...with breakfast at six and early church.

April 22: Mike was horrified when he wheeled up at eight o'clock to find me a windblown wreck. We then...had more breakfast while the two [Tipton and Smith] decided how best to get us married this day. I thought I'd better let E.M.R. run the show, so he took me into Andover [4 miles from Thruxton] to my funny little hotel. At about three I decided to dress for my wedding at four. Mike had been gone so long I thought he must have obtained the license and was busy picking out flowers. I looked out the window at the town hall clock and suddenly felt very lonely, thinking of all the other brides an hour before their ceremony. But alas he was unsuccessful and we went for a long walk, both feeling quite let down.

April 23: On Monday evening I accompanied Mike to the vicarage.... My civilian clothes seemed to impress him [the vicar] of my status as a free agent. No success.

April 24: Each day I spend sewing, waiting for Mike. Each night we spend wandering about that damned little town – each night blue and sad over our plight. I hate the miserable hotel. Air raids every night with sirens to awaken the dead.

April 25: We had dinner at the White Mart with Major Smith. He really can offer no specific aid. At about this point I was giving up. Mike meantime was receiving all sorts of comments from the boys as to his posture, etc. etc.

April 26: Lt. Col. Tipton and Jeannie had dinner with us [Ann and Mike] at the Kimpton Café.... They brought us back to the hotel where we waited for the return of Jeannie. The people were thinking all the worst of Mike and me. I was very nervous with him in my room and made him go downstairs. We sat amidst countless cockroaches and died all kinds of death – so we went up again. When Jeannie arrived at two [AM] the alarm [sirens] started up again and the entire household wanted to know what was going on.

April 27: In the morning we got Wallbridge to drive us back to camp.

At the end of April Ann went to see her brother, Jim Little. Captain Brown, from the 436th Troop Carrier Group stationed in Membury, offered to take her to East Anglia to visit him. It was Ann's first ride in an airplane. She describes her adventure in her next two diary entries and more fully in her "Letters to Sara," written 40 years later:

Diary, April 30: I had a ride in an L-5 up to JBL's station. I surprised him no end by telephoning him from the control tower in the middle of the afternoon.

"Letters to Sara": I got myself all dressed in best uniform, and with small Musette bag with extra duds climbed into the L-5 aircraft. He [Capt. Brown] said to be careful not to put my heel through the floor! He said to step on the framework!! I couldn't believe it. The darned thing was made of canvas. All the little villages with church steeples were very picturesque and I was just settling down to enjoying the countryside when he banked very steeply and scared me to death. He was <u>landing</u>! I didn't see any reason for this maneuver and thought he was showing off or something. At any rate, upon arrival I telephoned Jim [Little]. "Where are you?" he asked. "I'm right on your base at Base Ops" says I.

He came and got me in a jeep. Explained that their outfit had lost two big bombers the day before, that the Red Cross Girls on the base were terribly upset and had sort of closed up for the day, but I could sleep in a room off the Mess Hall which had been set up for some girls imported from London, there for the Saturday night dance.

Jim took me around to see the "War Room" (he was an intelligence officer, 90-day wonder type), introduced me to his boss and took me to the evening dance.

When I first got into the room set aside for the Limeys [common slang for the Brits], I had found about ten or eleven cots. One girl was already there in the afternoon and I asked sweetly if there was any particular order as to where one slept. She just sort of shrugged indifferently, so I chose the single cot at the very end of the room which was the only one not lined up on either side of the room, and just put my musette bag in it to reserve it. When I came back, hours later, it was blackout, of course.

I entered the building, heard general conversation going on in the dark room, male voices intermingling with the giggles. So I sort of stood in the doorway and said "A-hem" a couple of times in fairly loud tone, then went to the bathroom to give everyone time to clear out. I lingered as long as I could and went back to the "dorm." No such thing. Same as before. What to do? Nothing. I did not know how to get hold of JBL, and even if I could what could he do? No hotels or inns out in that black countryside. So I just proceeded to my little cot, pulled up the cover and undressed a la upper berth and hoped no one would find me. I must say "it" was going on all night long and I didn't know whether to laugh or cry, but I was so tired I just fell asleep.

Early the next morning I heard the big planes taking off and climbing higher and higher getting into formation for a bombing mission. I thought to

Jim Bellows Little in uniform

myself, who do you think you are to criticize such goings-on as of the night before?

At breakfast I told JBL about my experience, and just like a brother he said, "Tsk. tsk. Were you the only one without a partner?" No Sympathy from him! When I went back to get my clothes I got into a conversation with one of the girls. They work for about $4.00 a week, come for the good food, cigarettes and silk stockings.

Diary, May 1: The trip back [to Membury] was only eleven hours long. I simply detest trains and have decided henceforth to travel only by air.

By late spring, Ann and Jeannie had been on several double dates with Mike and Jim Tipton. Mike reminded Jim of his brother Tip, who always did well with the ladies, so he didn't mind Mike and his exploits. He wasn't too concerned about Miss Little either; in his experience, women that joined the Red Cross hostess units must have known what they were signing up for. Like Mathilda before him, he assumed she was no virgin. He did worry about Jeannie though. She was compliant and loving and he bristled whenever Miss Ann Little got too bossy with her.

When Colonel Meyer was reassigned elsewhere, Jim Tipton became interim commander for the group, but he was really hoping to get his own outfit soon. If he did get shipped out, he would miss Jeannie, though he knew it was just as well. His wife back home was writing letters that were beginning to worry him, he had a war to fight and these women were only a distraction. A complicated affair he did not need. As it happened, Ann's memorable first ride in an airplane coincidentally occurred on the same day Lt. Colonel Jim Tipton was interviewing for his second command.

Chapter 21

INTO THE THICK OF IT

Jim Tipton assumed his second command on May 7th, 1944. In his 1982 memoir he writes about the circumstances:

> When General Weyland called me in to interview for the 363rd command, my remarks were just that, "I'll do the best I can."
>
> "Tipton," he said, "When you meet your maybe new boss, tell him you're the best fighter commander there ever was or will be."
>
> I gathered this was the only way to interview for a job..., which I wanted very much, incidentally. "I'll be damned if I'll make such a ridiculous remark," I told myself. They take me as I am or else...which illustrates that stiff-necked reserve I seldom seem to control, or want to; even when the rewards are great.

Apparently General "Tex" Sanders, the 100th Fighter Wing Commander of the Ninth Air Force, decided the young officer was good enough. Jim Tipton took over command of the 363rd and was promoted to Colonel, a "full bird," by May 30th. It was a dream come true: he was the commander of a P-51 group, a Mustang unit.

Jim writes further about his impressions in his memoir, switching to third person:

> [He was] on his way to join his new outfit at Staplehurst Airfield, not far from Maidstone, in Kent, the garden spot of Jolly old England. He is delighted to go. Command held no terrors for him (I told you he was dumb) and the P-51 was the best flying machine in the world. There would be no problem in check-out; the 51 was a single engine, stick and rudder airplane, wasn't it? No sweat.

He goes on to describe his new situation:

> The 363rd was flying from a temporary landing strip built with a little bit of "chicken wire" and a lot of engineering ingenuity. It was disconcertingly rough and noisy on takeoff and landing. Taxying was particularly painful; S-ing along to keep the nose

clear, bouncing and swaying side to side, the stuff [PSP, pierced steel plank] just ruffling up in front of you; wondering if the beautiful thing [P-51] could stand the punishment. One time it didn't. My left gear slowly collapsed and there was nothing I could do about it. Embarrassing.

The 363rd Fighter Group in the Ninth Air Force consisted of 3 squadrons of 16 Mustangs, 48 in all, strategically placed on an airfield close to the English Channel. Tactical groups usually got their orders from Wing Command the night before and on the evening of May 29th word came down that the entire group was scheduled to rendezvous with a B-17 bomber unit on a deep escort. The next morning one of the squadron leaders informed his new commander that none of his P-51s had yet been given "legs" and they couldn't fly the distance. There was no time to fix it and Jim Tipton lost his famous temper, outraged that he had not been informed before. He felt certain he could have gotten some auxiliary fuel tanks on those planes if he had known, but there was no time and they had to go out 16 fighters short.

More excerpts from Jim's memoir:

As lead, I took off first. Rattling down that bumpy, noisy runway I eased into full throttle and all hell broke loose. White smoke poured past, clatter and explosions, and vibration much worse than the banging from the chicken wire runway. It felt as if the aircraft would shake itself to pieces and me with it. I went into shock. Had never experienced anything like that before, pulled back on the throttle with abort in mind. The engine caught and smoothed out at about cruise RPM. By this time we were well down the so-called runway and [I] decided that trying for takeoff speed was safer then ditching. It flew.

By the time the group – 2 squadrons – had cleared the runway, so I could return my sick bird, I had changed my mind once again. We already were 16 aircraft short, all our recent escort missions had been milk runs, and my engine wasn't missing a tick at cruise throttle; ergo, we go....

Two hours or so later we eased into position with our big friends and sighted a gaggle of mixed Germans. Fate. My second time to see Jerry airborne...and I was there only because our commitment was one squadron short.

Could have been, should have been a beautiful bounce. The Hun was in a loose helter-skelter stream of fighters of all types in a uniform diving left turn; apparently to an attack position below our bombing formation. We must have interrupted them. They seemed more bent on getting away, rather than seriously attacking the B-17s.

In the excitement I forgot my temperamental engine and went into combat throttle. The reminder was loud and clear. Back to cruise throttle and once again the engine stabilized. A diving turn positioned us dead astern, and close behind, what appeared to be the trailing aircraft of the formation. Identified as a ME 410 by the gun camera later, it was going away rather rapidly. Fired one burst, a short one I think; dead center hits.

By the time I turned away from the wounded ME 410, I could see no bandits behind, and the untidy formation of MEs and FWs had all but disappeared down and away; too fast for my sick bird.... I wanted to get all the altitude I could get, at least until we had the English Channel back in sight. At the time of the attack the bombers were about 25,000 feet, much much closer to Berlin than to the coast, and still penetrating...scared me to death and confirmed the obvious fact that only a damn fool would fly deep in GAF [German Air Force] airspace with a monkey wrench in his carburetor.

That was Jim Tipton's first confirmed kill and earned him a swastika on the side of his Mustang, a P-51 named Diablo in honor of his little black cocker spaniel back home. That day his group, even with 16 short, scored 12 enemy aircraft destroyed.

In his 1985 USAF "Oral History" (p. 35-36), Jim talks about the escort work done by the 363rd and how he was feeling about it at the time:

I knew it was important, and obviously people were dying...for example, escorting those bombers on the straight and level over their bomb runs, [there was] all that flak all over the place. You could practically get out and walk on it. It was serious. There is no question about it. You felt sorry when you would see those bombers knocked down. You would get a hit every once in a while yourself. You didn't know if you were going to get out of that trip or not. After all, we were a bunch of kids just having a ball, fighting a war.

He loved the fight and he loved the air. He writes about flying his Mustang Diablo in his 1982 memoir:

We flew and we kept flying. The P-51 was a pilot's airplane. We learned to bomb with it – good ole tactical air support – and to strafe. But our prime mission was air superiority – to win the air battle. The P-51 was well endowed for this role. Can't remember how many long range escort missions I flew, but remember rather vividly how many I did not fly: I did not fly the day after a long mission. The P-51 cockpit was great, but a 6' 2" frame and 35" legs were just a bit much when airborne time was 5 hours or better. (I remember one mission over Berlin which exceeded 7 hours.) Not being able to stretch my legs straight, I sat on my hip bones for the duration and had to be lifted out of the cockpit, numb and paralyzed. It would take a day or two to reduce the soreness sufficiently to fly again. Many methods were suggested to cope with the pain. I tried them all; different isometric exercises, sitting on slick magazines like a Saturday Evening Post (so to slide around easily). The one which worked best for me was to sit perfectly still until absolutely numb, then I could ignore it. It didn't seem to affect the rudder work.

Speculation about the [Normandy] invasion was rampant my first month with the 363rd. When and where the surface forces would strike were well kept secrets, but preparations were obvious. Intensive counter air operations and increased emphasis on interdiction...virtually presented the fighter units carte blanche for attacking targets of opportunity. On the return leg from escorting bombers we often would drop down to look for likely targets.... My second aircraft confirmed was a D 217 destroyed on an airfield hidden in a forest somewhere in Germany.

Incidentally, we were quite familiar with the buzz-bomb. Our airstrip evidently was squarely below a major flight path between continental launch pads and London. We could see and hear them go over by day and, mostly, at night. The "Ack-Ack" surrounding us was deafening, and apparently not too effective.... We were fortunate. Several were dumped quite close, but we suffered no damage. I know we discussed using our Mustangs to intercept [them].... We speculated it might be fun, but scary, to upset the autopilot by flipping it on its back with one's own wingtip – but I believe we left it to the RAF.

In his memoir, Jim gets a little defensive about the 363rd and its role as the rearguard tactical Mustang unit, which had less opportunity to participate in high profile aerial "dogfights," but he first allows himself a trace of braggadocio, so very rare for James Baird Tipton:

I had the utmost confidence in my ability as a pilot and a gunner. One can't really want war's destruction, death and the aftermath, if one had a choice. But being given a war, there is very little reason not to enjoy it. I had dreamed and schemed over half my life about pursuit/fighter aircraft and there I was, thrust into an almost idealistic situation. I had been in love with guns, shooting and hunting from a tender age – my father's influence – and had at home a formidable collection of shotguns and rifles. I thought I could outfly and outshoot just about anything: those 6-each 50-caliber guns and the gunsight in the 51 were fantastic.

Keep in mind that people under war-stress (and pilots all the time, I think) have a built-in conviction in fate. One doesn't worry too much about things he can't control and you sure can't control malevolent ground fire. At high and medium altitudes the little dark flowers blossomed above, below, in front or beside us, all of it unexpectedly expected.... At low altitudes [there were] tiny flashes or gleaming globs, seemingly slowly streaming by like this long waterfall in reverse.

Probably the most disconcerting thoughts about low altitude attacks was wondering about the weapons firing [up] at us we couldn't see – no tracer or muzzle blast. There was, of course, no way to anticipate or avoid a shell or a round already fired. One could only hope for a lousy gunner and fly a crooked track to confuse him, all the while wondering if your evasive maneuvers might not be compensating for his bad aim by turning into a gratuitous hit.

I've never heard of a fighter pilot intentionally landing his aircraft to attack a ground target. By an overwhelming majority the sorties of 9th AF fighters in WW2 contained pilots _flying_ (flying!) against ground targets, many of them hazardous and all of them requiring a modicum of pilot skill and discipline for success.

When one was in the same airspace with enemy aircraft, flack is nil to nonexistent, another bonus. Air to air is the hunt; approached almost like a sporting event. But you'll have to admit air to air is the glamour and the fun, whereas the other type mission is hard work and dedication – logistics and maintenance as well as operations – with very little glory. But my, how effective! What I'm trying to say is that flying a combat mission is aerial combat whatever the target. For me, I'll say it takes as much skill and a lot more pucker to successfully attack ground targets made difficult by terrain, defenses, and munitions configurations. There should be some way to glamorize the dive bomber, ship bomber, strafer, rocketeer, and such. And don't ask me how to do this either; I'm a reader, not a writer.

Chapter 22

D-DAY AND OTHER DISTRACTIONS

In early May, Ann Little was still in Membury with the 436th and still seeing Mike, stationed with the 366th in Thruxton. Jeannie was still with Jim Tipton, though he and his 363rd group were twice as far away, in Staplehurst. The sergeant and the colonel would often carpool, Jim picking up Mike on his way to see Jeannie. Thruxton was the halfway point and it broke up the long trip. Besides, he was no longer Mike's commander and had come to enjoy the sergeant's company: Mike was a nice enough guy, though Jim couldn't understand what Ann Little saw in him.

Ann Little's diary entries concerning E.M.R. May through June 6th, 1944, D-Day:

May 5: Dear Diary: During the course of the dance Molly told me there was a call for me so when I went around the corner at the end of the canteen, I bumped smack into Mike! Wasn't that lovely. A little English WAAF spent the night in Jeannie's bed. Mike and I sat up until all hours smooching. Ah me.

May 15: Got off to Thruxton... Mike and I had dinner [at the] Kimpton Café. 'Twas there that he presented me with a wedding ring to wear on my right hand until the day when he will place it where it belongs.

May 19: In the afternoon Jeannie and I decorated the club.... By about 5:30 I was licked – however, with a nap, bath, egg and drink, I arrived at the dance in fine shape. Mike added a decoration in the form of a Paper Doll hung over the orchestra, which started things off with the tune ["Paper Doll," their special song]. Late in the evening I became annoyed with E.M.R. and removed my ring.

May 26: Opened up for the dance, which I did not attend. Mike came to see me, but I was not very nice to him.

June 6: After a luxurious breakfast in bed I went [to a salon] and had a permanent to the tune of $22.00, including tip!! After lunch at Grosvenor House, and a bit of shopping, I went back to the hotel and awaited Mike. I had an awful feeling he would not be able to come. But at five o'clock he called me and we had about twelve beautiful hours together. We dined and wined and talked half the night. This was D-Day and back at camp Jeannie "sweated it out" all night.

D-Day as described by Jim Tipton in his 1982 memoir:

When the invasion (Operation Overlord) finally came, 9th Air Force and XIX TAC [Tactical Air Command] established the role of the 363rd for the next 3 months.... The 354th [Mustang] Group became the hunter ranging far in advance, seeking the enemy before he could attack. We became the watchdog, the reserve in the rear to fend against wolves.... For the most part our role consisted of monotonous patrols over the crowded sea routes crossing the channel and over the beachheads.

Let me insert here quite clearly that my words are not critical concerning these roles. We were envious, not demented. Higher headquarters were almost pathological in their fears of what might happen to the armada at its most fragile moments seeking a foothold in France.

Like a Monday morning quarterback, it looks less complicated now; it wasn't then. Into the unknown, not knowing what opposition awaited the all-out effort – which must succeed or else. Precautions were taken to counter any and all contingencies. One of these contingencies resulted in an unusual and hair-raising experience for the 363rd.

We took off early on D-Day morning in group formation, garish in our new war paint of black and white zebra stripes; designed to enhance identification. Our task was to provide armed escort for the airborne army en route to drop zones behind beachheads in Normandy. Flying low to avoid radar, we rendezvoused before dawn with a long column of C-47s (in Vs of three) tugging gliders, heading south over the Channel. They were almost on the deck [ground] making headway of not much more than 100 knots, if that. We wanted to stay low as well, to avoid radar. We throttled back to near landing speed and made huge serpentine maneuvers to keep pace with the convoy. Most difficult.

Somewhere just south of the English coast...we were less than 60 miles from enemy radar and drawing closer by the minute.

Maneuvers were also restricted laterally; we wanted to avoid being shot at by our own naval forces who herded the hordes of ships and landing craft which dotted the sea. Most of the time, in our exaggerated sine-curve progress toward the DZ [drop zone], we passed under the column of C-47s [including the cables on the gliders]. But not always. Quite soon our slow maneuvering had broken up [our] Group into 3 separate squadrons, and possibly into elements and flights.

It was a rat race to end all rodent competition! P-51s began popping up from every quarter. Cramped within our prescribed air corridor, we found ourselves meeting friends head on, pulling over, diving under, and wondering where the next Mustang would appear unexpectedly at full front quadrant. Fortunately, friendly fire was avoided and no enemy aircraft was sighted. We were so busy looking for each other and keeping a weather eye on the transports that I doubt if the Hun would have been identified had he joined one of our elements. We didn't ruffle a feather, but we could have; we probably hold the record for most near miss air collisions in the shortest period of time.

This type of escort was not repeated to my knowledge. There was no reason for an encore because there were no more largescale airborne operations until the allied forces were on the threshold of Germany 3½ months later. And there was no requirement for close escort such as described above because there was no further need for secrecy; landing forces told all the world when and where the Allies would invade the continent.

Moreover, the GAF didn't react to the invasion in an all-out confrontation as was expected. In fact, they held back and made no air attacks worthy of name against landing forces, make-shift harbors full of shipping, or the continuous stream of transports crossing the Channel. Most strange.

D-Day, June 6th, was only the beginning of one of the "largest amphibious military assaults in history." Subsequently, towards the end of the month and after the peninsula was considered secure, both the 366th P-47 Thunderbolt fighters and the 363rd P-51 Mustangs would be moved to France.

Both boyfriends would soon be gone. Jeannie was inconsolable when Colonel Tipton left on the 9th of July for the Maupertus-sur-Mer

Airfield (A-15) in Normandy, but Ann was more resolute than sad when Mike had left her two weeks earlier.

Ann Little knew of a high school sweetheart in Mike Regond's past. According to him, the woman didn't mind if he dated other women while away in the ETO. The way he put it, it made perfect, logical sense. He was essentially free and could straighten things out when they got back home. He had told Ann about the arrangement on March 22nd over snifters of brandy. He was already spoken for; that and the fact that she was saving herself for marriage were her best arguments for protecting her maidenhead.

But the visit to East Anglia had begun to percolate into her mind. The fitful night on the cot, followed by seeing those dear soldier-boys gearing up to meet their death early the next day, made her meager atonement to Mike seem insufficient. Her "reputation" seemed frivolous compared to what he was putting on the line to keep her safe from those crazy Nazis. She had already begun to relent.

After the dizzying buildup to D-Day, life at Membury began to return to normal, except everything was different. The English meadows were bright with summer wildflowers, the Allies were successfully flexing their muscle and though war was grim, there was a willful delight in every step Ann took. Mike was saying and doing all the right things, and when it became obvious he would be relocated soon, her urgency deepened. Every day and every evening they would plot to meet; their trysts became more intense; every goodbye more wrenching. Her wiring was strung tight, like a bow with an arrow. She was feeling desperate, reckless love. Mike had gotten a place for her to stay closer to Thruxton. She writes about the next eight days in her diary:

June 20: This was the day I arrived at Mrs. Logles – a new establishment that Mike found for me. Mr. Logels looks surprisingly like Doc [her commander], especially around the eyes. They are a very cute old couple who, when in doubt, suggest a cup of tea. I took a very long nap in the afternoon and consequently did not sleep at all well.

June 21: We [Mike and Ann] went to the Morris and had dinner. I guess that's all we did. Ho Hum.... I went shopping with Mrs. Logels – our expedition was very fruitful inasmuch as I purchased a lot of things for the club. I love my little room at Mrs. Logels and slept like a kitten.

June 22: We [Mike and Ann] spent the day sitting in the sun talking – I left Thruxton at about five in the evening in order to be in Tent City in time to teach French.... Upon my return to the club I was overcome with blue eyes at the thought of my departing Michael.

June 23: Having made up a lovely mental barrier to keep my secret thoughts and feelings from the public eye, it is not hard to imagine into how many pieces I broke when Mike arrived at Membury! For about half an hour I could not even greet him properly because I was so surprised to see him.... Mike left at midnight.

June 24: At about 9 I set sail for Thruxton to visit E.M.R. who asked me to come today instead of tomorrow. He expects to go [to France] at any

Ann and Mike, during their stay with Mrs. Logel and looking as though they had "swallowed a canary"

moment. Arrived at Mrs. Logels, who had a cup of tea ready.

June 25: Michael persuaded me to stay over today. I called Tuffy [one of her ARC staff] to ease my conscience. She said everything was very quiet and for me to not worry or to hurry. So here I am again at Mrs. Logel's. Mike is watching me write in my diary. We went to Ashbury to dinner in a very quaint hotel. The George....

June 26: I arrived back in camp in time for a chicken dinner. Col. Williams said I looked as though I had swallowed a canary. As a matter of fact, that's just how I felt. I can't remember what happened the rest of the day....

Mike had told her he loved her and needed her, would do anything to marry her, but it had been hard to bear when she discovered his duplicity. Discovery had come too late. She had already given him everything he wanted and would gladly have given more.

June 27: .... In the afternoon after lunch at the Maison Basque, I did shopping etc. Saw a movie – "French without Tears" – upon my return…I found that Mike was still there so I went to see him. I learned that it was his 10th wedding anniversary. It threw me off. But not for long. Ahem.

June 28: Wednesday Mike appeared as I thought he might. We both seemed a little overwrought by all this on again off again business of his leaving. Mr. Ray had put in a few words about my neglect of the club, faulty reports etc. etc. and altogether I was upset and tired. My emotions were strained further by words from Mike which I am afraid sent me to bed in tears.

June 29: …. He learned that he was to leave at an early hour the next morning, so we said goodnight rather early. After all this there was really not much to say except just that and God speed.

She couldn't believe how they had left it. Ann earmarked her diary by clipping off the bottom corners of the last three pages in June, 1944. The entries began on Sunday, with "Michael persuaded me to stay over today" and ended Thursday with "that and God speed." After the incredible high of feeling truly loved, she had stupidly caught him unawares on his "big" wedding anniversary. She regretted seeing him trying to hide that letter as she watched those crazy expressions working across his face.

When he had come around again the next day with the note "Please say YES!" written a thousand times, she only wished she had said "No!" a thousand times. She had been too weary to smile and didn't know what to do or how to feel. Like an open blister, she was emptied and raw.

Ann dwelled on a recent conversation she'd had with one of the D-Day pilots, who was repulsed with what happened to the U.S. paratroopers that didn't make it. She was told they were found strung up in the very trees that had caught them, secured there with barbed wire, their throats slit open. Mike had been only slightly better to her (at least she was still breathing), but he had turned her into a POW swinging from a branch for everyone to see. Her brain couldn't stop that image, along with their song, "Paper Doll," both spooling in a mindlessly eternal loop.

She ruefully tried to amuse herself with a pun aimed at his wife's legitimate status versus her own. Apparently he really preferred a "doll with papers" to call his own, instead of her. She braced herself to go face the boys in the canteen. She forced a smile to cover her mouth; they deserved it.

In just a few short months she had allowed herself to be drawn into a wartime romance that was just that. She'd been acting like she was Ingrid Bergman and he was Humphrey Bogart, all caught up in the throes of some unrequited love; stupid, simpleminded, less than worthy Ann and her childish fancies. She couldn't have known at the time that her two daughters would hear her singing the "Paper Doll" tune well into her 80s.

Chapter 23

FRENCH LANDSCAPES

Before and after the D-Day invasion there was a top secret tactical operation in place called "Fortitude." The Allied forces wanted to keep the Nazis' focus away from France by targeting red herrings close to the Fatherland. The campaign's objective was to suggest to Germany that Norway and Calais were the Allies' real targets and it had worked beautifully. The Nazi strategists were convinced that the invasion of Normandy was only a diversion and not what it actually was – the juggernaut that would push them back on their heels.

In Jim Tipton's memoir he reminisces about his unit's next move, from Staplehurst to the Maupertus Airstrip in Cherbourg, France, where he had two memorable visits from two famous WW2 generals. The first visit was from General Lewis H. Brereton, who wrote an after-the-fact accounting of his memories in WW2, the *Brereton Diaries,* published in 1946 by William Morrow. Jim Tipton told it this way:

> For some reason, I ferried the last P-51 from Staplehurst to Cherbourg. I remember the flight because I "beat-up" our Kent airfield in salute and goodbye – an infraction of rules similar to the incident two months earlier [where I] sent Lt. Carr packing... a direct violation of flying regulations.

> Many of the 9th Air Force fighter units were operating out of Normandy before the 363rd moved to its first base in France. The engineers had done an excellent job with the facilities and we soon found ourselves with hard surface runways, taxiways and parking spaces. The Germans had abandoned the base with surprisingly negligible destruction. The damage we found was probably from Allied attacks rather than from German efforts to make the base untenable. Compared to the hastily built wire-mesh flying strips and tent cities of other units in Normandy, we were in hog heaven.

> One unsought, unwanted bonus of "owning" the only Allied Airdrome in France worthy of the name was providing landing facilities for distinguished visitors. We didn't relish the time lost on the thankless task of playing host.

General Brereton's visit I remember well. He made an impression on me – not favorable; although I must admit that the incident was probably due to my lack of tact and poor communications. I treated General Brereton as any other VIP. I did not consider him in my chain of command. At the time we were assigned to XIX TAC and its wing while under operational control of General Quesada's XI TAC.

Units, in short order, were living, working and relaxing in permanent type buildings, many of them having been repaired using ye old American ingenuity. As Gen. Weyland explained later, "Any damn fool can live uncomfortably." The extra effort reaped huge benefits, not only in comfort, but pride, esprit, morale and, not least, preempting idle hands and minds. I was rather proud of the results. The men had pitched in and had made a lot out of a little and I was showing it off like a proud papa.

So I burbled along about my points of interest, trying to span time with this remote individual methodically wrapped around himself. Having viewed several renovation projects, I interpreted a chance remark as a request to see an example of battle damage. We dismounted [from the jeep] to look at a German barracks building with one end blown off by a shell.

The following day I received a phone call from Wing saying the 9th AF commander had reported through channels that the 363rd Group was living under substandard conditions in bombed out buildings. So much for my articulate tour guide talents...he was to me a distinguished visitor, one of many, and not an inspector as his [post-war] book would imply.

Colonel Tipton's other famous visitor was General George S. Patton, Jr., the man who would lead the United States Third Army after the June 4th Normandy invasion. In recounting this story, my father commented on how unexpectedly high Patton's voice was. It did not sound at all like actor George C. Scott's Oscar-winning portrayal of the man. He talks about their brief face-to-face encounter before the push to Germany, when Jim and his fighter group helped support Patton and his infantrymen:

Pictures of the General reminded me of why he was there. Gen. Patton was under wraps at the time and not yet approved as CG [Commanding General] of the 3rd Army. I wasn't a party to the planning, but later it was obvious that the Secretary of War wanted an eyeball confrontation [with Patton] before he would agree to imposing him over the defenseless GIs.

Patton had leapt into news prominence a short time before by slapping a GI in Italy, thus his presence in Normandy was a potential news item for our news hounds as well as a piece of military intelligence, probably important for the Germans. Mr. Stimson's [the Secretary of War] arrival was delayed and General Patton was stoic, even morose. At least he wasn't given to humor, which is the basic reason that made his visit memorable. He told this story which I believed then to be a true one.

General Patton, while fighting Rommel in Africa, met a tribe of Bedouins native to that particular part of the Sahara. His objective was to drop them behind the enemy to [disrupt] Rommel's communications. They were eager to fight the Germans, particularly

General Patton visiting with Colonel Tipton and the 363rd in Normandy

with equipment and munitions supplied by the Americans, but were hesitant about jumping out of the C-47s. Finally, after quite a bit of haggling and conversation amongst themselves, they agreed [to jump if the] aircraft flew at 200 feet instead of 300 feet. Patton explained that at 200 feet the parachute opening would be critically dangerous.

Patton: "What's the objection to 300 feet?"

Bedouin: "What are parachutes?"...was the incredible answer.

Those fighters were willing to jump out of the aircraft with guns and knives and nothing else, like leaping off the back of their camels. If [General Patton] was pulling my leg, he succeeded marvelously well. I believed him then, I believe him now. However, I've never heard or read this story since. If it were true there must have been staff members and interpreters with General Patton at the time of the conference [with the Bedouins] who would have repeated it.

Colonel Tipton remained at the French post, known as A-15, until a bombardment group moved in and he took his group over to Azeville, or A-7, on August 22. Originally built as a temporary airstrip, the accommodations were basic, but adequate, with a single wire mesh airstrip and minimal infrastructure and communications.

Chapter 24

THE LANGUAGE OF LOVE

While Jim Tipton found himself being confounded by visitors on the coast of France in Cherbourg, Ann Little had been back in Membury, missing Mike in bursts, even as she steeled herself not to. Soon enough she was back at it: finding girls, throwing parties, calling bingo, cleaning the canteen, drinking too much, taking naps; chatting up the boys, watching movies, attending church, playing bridge, drinking too much, sleeping in; going to London, ordering supplies, dancing with officers, working the staff, drinking too much and falling into bed early if she could. At least she wasn't acting sorry for herself. She had applied to the ARC headquarters in London for reassignment to France shortly after Mike had left. She needed to find him. She needed to remind him of who he really loved.

Despite no Mike, one of the bright spots that July was a gala given by the wing commanders for the 436th Group at the The Chequers Hotel in close-by Newbury. For the event, Ann went over to Rook's nest

Ann Little dressed for a dance

and borrowed an evening gown with matching jewelry. She arrived at the big formal party in a long black net sheath with a jade green sash pulled tight around her 24" waist. She knew she would never be a natural beauty, but she had her moments. When she glanced at herself in one of the gilded full length mirrors placed strategically around the dance floor, she knew this was one of those moments. Even she had to admit the overall effect was attractive. Jane would be impressed with her little sister.

She was escorted there and back by the base CO, Colonel Williams, as was his due as the commander. He told her four times during the night that she was the prettiest girl there. He was an old schoolmate of Jeannie's sweetheart, Colonel Tipton, and everyone called him "Doc." He was from Kentucky and acted gentlemanly and sympathetic towards her when he took her home; he didn't press her for more than a friendly kiss. She thought it was a good reflection on Tipton to have such a courtly friend, though "El Colonel" hadn't been coming around much lately – ever since he had become a busy group commander. She hoped he was worthy of Jeannie and not taking advantage of her friend's naivety.

Life as an ARC director kept Ann busy enough. She was authoritative when she needed to be, especially one night when the whole orchestra got drunk and she had to kick two "commandos" out of the canteen, or the day when she fired one of her kitchen help for truancy. By the end of August she got word she was going to France and was glad of it; the needed transfer couldn't have come too soon.

The impetus behind her strategy to get the new assignment involved her "special talent." At last her French was an asset she could parley into a new position. She would miss Doc and her three kittens, Fit-Fit and Fit and Fit-Fit-Fit. But not her direct supervisor, Mr. Fey – he was a prick. She decided to place the kittens with Mrs. Spotteswood, at Rooks Nest, where she knew they'd always be warm.

These are Ann Little's diary entries concerning her relocation in 1944:

August 25: My last dance at the Aero Club. The drummer boy made a speech about me which turned my knees to cotton and then I had to speak a little piece too. My message was to treat Jeannie especially kindly as she would run the club alone. Later I found that a staff assistant is to be sent to her. Wonder what she'll be like. The early part of my day was spent in packing and I find now that I did it all wrong. O tempora – O mores!

August 26: This long and full day started off with a little trip into London. I accomplished my errands in jig time and was back at camp about 3 o'clock. To my amazement, surprise and pleasure, I found that I was to be assigned to Colonel Tipton's outfit! Poor Jeannie looked more chagrined than ever, although she realized full well that such an arrangement would never have done for her.

My drinking for the day consisted of sherry, rum, gin, brandy, champagne and back to brandy. Well, the only thing I missed was whiskey! I had a wonderful time dancing with the Col. [Williams]. In the end it was Jeannie who got high! She was so cute about it.

August 27: Got myself to the appointed place at the appointed hour only to wait...for five solid hours. Finally I arranged for a trip over with Col. Williams and went back to camp.

August 28: Whatta day. The Col. – "Isn't Doc the sweetest man" – brought me to my new home. At least this is where I am hanging my hat.

In England the Aero Clubs were in a fixed location, but Ann had been forewarned at headquarters that in France the ARC girls traveled with their outfit. She was leaving the stationary comfort of Membury and joining a movable city of olive-drab canvas tents, where all arrangements had to be done on site. Digging latrines, erecting shelters, stringing electricity, supplying water, assembling gas stoves, rolling out the pierced metal sheeting for a landing strip – everything was portable.

On the flight to France, Ann was relaxed. She had gotten used to flying and enjoyed the Ferris wheel perspective as they tipped wing and began the spiral descent down towards the recently constructed airfield. She smiled as Colonel Tipton came into view, sitting on the fender of his jeep, one long leg propped up on the bumper. As usual, he looked like a movie star, with his white silk Air Corps ascot floating out behind him on the wind. When she climbed out of the aircraft she charged right over, extending her hand, surprising him with, "I'm your new Red Cross Girl!"

From Jim Tipton's 1982 memoir:

I do remember meeting a C-47 which had landed on the strip. Communications had alerted me that Colonel Adrial "Doc" Williams, a fellow member of my Flying Cadet Class 39'B and commander of one of the troop carrier groups, was the pilot. It was nice to see him. He was ferrying Red Cross canteen supplies from England to our new base. Also aboard was a Red Cross Girl whom I had met on [Christmas Eve]. I supposed she knew what she was facing: tent city, mud, and no modern convenience. Surely an adventurous spirit.

After exchanging news from England, mostly about Jeannie and E.M.R., Colonel Tipton delivered Ann to her field tent. It was a total wreck inside, with all surfaces covered in feminine mayhem. Under all the fluff, she noted two dressers arranged beside a handsome three-panel dressing screen, no doubt all "liberated" from the abandoned estate she could see across the way. She did not approve of stealing from civilians. She cleared off one of the cots before she went out to meet with Colonel Tipton. He seemed unusually animated that day, even talkative. When she returned to her tent, it was dusk and there was still no one there.

She opened the tent's flap door as wide as she could and curled into her sleeping bag, which she had earlier put on the bed with the least amount of clutter. She luxuriated in the cool air drifting in and gazed out at the ruined French estate house. It was in shadowed profile at the far tip of an overgrown field. As the waxing moon revealed more detail, Ann placed the structure's architecture in the Renaissance Period and noticed she was looking at the old manor from the edge of a once formal garden. There were traces of a wide esplanade with sweeping avenues tilting away from it, like turning spokes trying to leave the abandoned chateau's hollow bastion behind.

Wandering, her mind led her into a half conscious sleep. When she felt her pretty calico kitty, "Fit Fit," start walking up her legs to cuddle, she reached out...until she remembered she wasn't in England anymore, but in a tent, in France. Looking into the dark, she thought she saw a rat and SHRIEKED as someone SHRIEKED back when Ann batted at a hand holding a stack of papers, which went flying into the face of the terrified woman who was groping around in the dark for her bed. The rattled girl was just trying to get some sleep. The loud commotion jerked everyone awake within earshot, which was everyone within miles. The new Red Cross girl had made quite an entrance into the 363rd.

The next day, Ann was heartened to find out the two messy occupants of her tent were not the unit's regular ARC girls, but two young French women who constituted the hired help. Within days a real Red Cross worker would return and she could get down to business.

In her diary, Ann wrote about her duties working under a new director in France:

August 31: Dorothy arrived last night and we had a hilarious time trying to fit everyone in. The tent was in a mess and about six officers descended upon us. They were all drunk and it ended up in a fight that I thought would bring down our little home around our ankles.

September 1: We spent the day working hard, moving and cleaning and arranging. My job is to be controller of the stores. Already short on sugar. The club really looks neat. We have lovely pale green canvas deck chairs, a piano radio Victrola, 2 ping pong tables, a very fancy red, white and blue bar. If the weather would stay mild, everything would indeed be perfect. I finished the day off with two shots of gin and went to bed feeling virtuous.

September 2: Hit a low today. It was grim as far as weather goes. I had cramps and felt lousy. After waking and making a not very valiant attempt at working, I folded and put in a little "sack time." This afternoon I feel much better. The club opened in fine style in the evening. We served coffee and donuts from 7:30 to 9:30. The two French gals got along fine. As for me, I have lost 17 lbs. of sugar. Oh me, Oh my.

September 3: This day was devoted to straightening out our tent. We now have a sitting room in one corner and sleeping place in another. Between are closets, etc. and a screen, to make it all very private. Now, if we only had running water everything would be just fine. Colonel Tipton went to see Jeannie today. Hope he brings back a pink pillow and a lot of letters from Michael. 'Twas 10 weeks ago today. Gee I'm blue.

Jim Tipton growing a beard, preparing to hand over his Mustang P-51, his second "Diablo," to reconnaissance; the abandoned chateau, at the Azeville airfield, in the background.

Within only three days of Colonel Williams dropping Ann off at the A-7 airfield in Normandy, Colonel Jim Tipton would leave the 363rd unit behind forever. It was being disbanded as a fighter group and he was bound to report for staff duty with the XIX TAC. The change of command seemed abrupt and Ann recalled that when Tipton met her at the airfield she had kidded him about needing a shave. He had gotten very serious about it and told her he was growing his stubble in protest. He didn't elaborate.

Chapter 25

A PARTRIDGE IN A PEAR TREE

After the Normandy invasion, Jim Tipton received confirmation that his short-lived marriage of nine months had been annulled. The letter came from the flying school at Foster Field, Texas, and the lawyer was careful to explain that "the allegations contained in it are the usual and formal ones used in a non-contested divorce." The charge was "abandonment." Colonel Tipton was too busy to let the wording upset him. He and Ann Abshier Weaver had been exchanging letters since he left Texas in December and he had been notified of the pending suit for divorce in late May. He had known it was coming, but the document still hit him hard, and he knew he would miss his little stepdaughter.

The official letter reads like this:

Ann Tipton vs J.B. Tipton in the district court of Victoria County, Texas, part 3:

That during the time Plaintiff and Defendant lived together as husband and wife as aforesaid she conducted herself with propriety, and at all times treated her said husband with kindness and forbearance. But the defendant, disregarding the solemnity of his marriage vow and his obligation to treat Plaintiff with kindness and attention, shortly after said marriage, commenced a course of unkind, harsh and tyrannical conduct toward her, which conduct continued with slight intermission until Plaintiff and Defendant finally separated on or about the 19th day of December, 1943. That on diverse occasions while Plaintiff lived with Defendant, as aforesaid, he was guilty of excesses, cruel treatment and outrages toward her, and of such a nature as to render their living together insupportable.

Timing is everything. The official divorce decree was written on July 18th, 1944. Jim must have received the document sometime in August. The news that he was no longer married may have spurred his decision to visit Jeannie in Membury on September 3rd. That visit would change Ann Little's life. He had known for some days he was losing the Mustang unit, his beloved P-51s, including Diablo. Those in charge had made their plans for him. Colonel Tipton had been in constant motion, reaching ever higher for his objectives, until the XIX TAC had stopped him in his tracks. He had time for visiting now. He had been turned into a desk drone.

As recorded in a *Wikipedia* article on the 363ʳᵈ Fighter Group when it was still tactical ("363d Expeditionary Operations Group"):

> In the two weeks following D-Day, the 363d [Fighter Group] experienced the most fruitful period of its service in the European Theater of Operations when patrols over France brought it actions with a total of 19 confirmed victories [aircraft destroyed]. However, a similar number of Mustangs were lost, albeit mostly to ground fire. During operations from the United Kingdom, the group was credited with 41 victories but lost 43 of its own aircraft in the process.

Like a knight on a chessboard, Colonel Tipton was being placed where command thought he could do the most good. By the time the 363ʳᵈ was located to Normandy's Azeville airfield, General Patton and General Stinson had come to terms and defined an outline for success. It was a solid strategy and involved redeploying the 363ʳᵈ Mustangs for reconnaissance work. The P-51 was more nimble than the heavier P-47 Thunderbolt, but its water-cooled engine made it more vulnerable too. Even though the air cooled "Bolt" was originally envisioned for high altitudes and the P-51 for close support, their roles got switched in practice. The Mustangs became the "eyes in the sky" for Patton, and the Thunderbolts were to be used as additional firepower for the Third Army and its bombers as Patton pushed through France, driving the Nazis backward.

In Jim Tipton's 1982 memoir he writes about losing the 363ʳᵈ Fighter Group:

> I believe I was the first fighter pilot to depart the 363ʳᵈ. I remember no ceremony, no goodbyes. I hope I thanked all the people who had worked closely with me. They deserved thanks and more. I don't see how the crews and the service groups did it; the unsung heroes. We fussed and fumed and were never satisfied, but even then, we knew they were doing a good job and patted them on the back once in a while – I hope. It was a sad day for me, leaving the essence of all I had wanted for quite some time, to become a non-combatant again.
>
> Can't remember when we were told the Fighter Group would be no more. I tend to believe that higher headquarters kept that se-

cret rather well. I think I learned about it just a few days before the event. This is the timeline:

1- The 363rd began moving from the Cherbourg post in Mon-tebourge (A-15) to the Azeville Airstrip (A-7) on 21 August, and flew its first mission from the site on 26 August.
2- Colonel Smelly, the new commander of the 363rd, arrived 27 August.
3- Assuming my 1951 WD66 is correct, I reported for duty with XIX TAC Hq. on 31 August
4- The 363rd Tactical Reconnaissance Group was born 4 September 1944.

Further clarification appears in Jim's USAF "Oral History" (p. 53):

The reason they wanted another reconnaissance unit was that the 9th Army was being activated. Each of the Armies had their tactical air command; the 9th TAC, the 19th, and the 29th. But the 29th didn't have a reconnaissance [unit], so the 363rd became one.

The following account is drawn from both the memoir and the "Oral History" (p. 49-50):

Permit me to record one last incident which...is illustrative of my talent for being misunderstood. It had to be within three weeks of departing the 363rd. I called on Gen Weyland in his mobile headquarters and "bearded" him. I explained...my feelings about being a supernumerary in his headquarters.... I kind of hemmed and hawed around like I always do, not very smart, not very tactful. He got red in the face and mad as hell.

Weyland: "Tipton, if you think I'm going to send you home with all these guys dying around here, you're wrong."

My mouth flopped open, eyes widened. Shock.

Tipton: "General, for God's sake, I don't want to be a recce pilot."

Weyland: "Don't worry. We don't want you to be a recce pilot."

I didn't know it at the time, but they took all of the fighter pilots out of the 363rd and scattered them throughout the 9th Air Force, except me; they put me in the 19th Tactical Air Command Head-quarters.

He thought I was trying to get out of his command, which I was; he thought I was trying to go home, which I wasn't.

> Tipton: "It took too long to get here. I want to go back to a fighter unit. I want to go out there where they are flying."

Weyland: Oh. Well. I'll see what I can do.

Colonel Jim Tipton was too high ranking to be put back into a cockpit assignment. He had to wait until a fighter group opened up, which it did, but the vacancy only happened because a unit lost its commander. His name was Colonel Cecil L. Wells and he was instantly killed when he hit his aircraft's clear hard canopy trying to bail out of his plane after taking flak. He was only 27 years old, and extremely well-liked by his men.

Colonel Jim Tipton assumed command of the 358th on September 20, 1944. When he took over the outfit the troops began calling him "Old Man Tipton," supposedly because of his "advanced age" of 29, and in deference to his predecessor, who really had died young. Likely too, he continued to earn this label with his hardnosed, straight-up de-meanor. He was "one tough hombre" according to Bert Lok, one of the ground crew who serviced the fighters' Thunderbolts. Bert also told me my father's arrival "lit a fire under the men."

After Tipton's former unit got their cameras installed, becoming the Reconnaissance Group for the 29th Army, Colonel Smelly and his men were quickly relocated to a village outside of Le Mans. On moving with the 363rd to her next station in France, Ann wrote about leaving Azeville in her diary:

September 11: The trip through Montebourge is still depressing. It was very sad to see an old man and woman working among the stones to gather together bits of their household. On the roads many people are walking or driving with all their worldly [goods].

September 13: At any rate we arrived in due course at our little tent, sans floor, sans light, sans anything. It is situated in a cow pasture with lots of you know what all over the place.... Dorothy and I went into Le Mans.... We had lamb chop dinner! My first in a year and was it good!

September 17: We went to church in the morning and I resolved not to be cross and irritable. It seems that the pressure of the work tends to make me snappy in my orders, for several people seem to take offence at my words.

September 18: Today we started our donut making. Everything went wrong from the field ranges not working on up.

September 19: I went swimming in the bright sunshine this afternoon. The water was very chilly, but it felt marvelous to be clean all over once again. My squeals amuse the French populace very much, not to mention the entire American Army!

September 21: Colonel Tipton came in with a bottle of Champagne which we did not take the time out to drink. He took a note from me to Michael saying I would be in Paris on Wed., the 27th.

Ann had been waiting in expectation of Colonel Tipton's return visit to the 363rd ever since he had given his Mustangs over to Reconnaissance just days after she'd arrived. When he handed her the champagne, he also mentioned the two pies he had noticed on Mike's cot. They both knew what that meant — no doubt a gift from some pretty French girl the sergeant had worked his charm on. Ann reacted with satirical nonchalance, "He has a way about him that language doesn't stop." Jim was glad Ann didn't take it too hard. He had no idea of what she was really feeling. He thought she was a "good sport."

When Colonel Smelly got word from Wing Command that the 363rd were to be relocated to Luxembourg, he told Ann and Dorothy, Ann's assistant, to go ahead and take two company jeeps into Paris while the new camp was being set up. It was just dumb luck that Colonel Tipton had come when he did, so Ann could get that note off to Mike. She was desperate to see him and now they could meet in her home-away-from-home, the "City of Lovers." She had sent him the dates and places of her itinerary. She assumed he would find his way.

Driving alone, Ann was alert with involuntary excitement. Mike had brought her along slowly, he never hurried their affair. He had been subtle with her seduction and had allowed her arousal to swell to the point where she became the aggressor, however clumsy. She had barely begun to give over to him when she found him on his bunk reading the love letter from his wife. Despite inner warnings, she still wanted more of him, she had only begun the surrender. Those supreme three days at Mrs. Logel's, consummated that last evening at the George Hotel, had been a painful tease. This meeting would be a test of everything she felt, and she hadn't seen Michael in months.

Ann Little had never approached Paris from the west. Long before reaching her destination in the loud, gyrating jeep, she watched as the gothic Cathedral of Our Lady rose up from the shimmery mirage created by the flat plains. The lovely vision made her feel weightless and clean, void of all emotions in the miracle of it. As she neared Chartres, the ornate façade reached higher and higher, until she completely lost sight of it in the city's tangle. It remained shrouded behind high walls and narrow corners as she navigated through the inner streets without ever glimpsing the "sanctuary of pilgrims" again, until she saw its two beckoning towers retreating in her rearview mirror.

She pushed on towards her meeting with E.M.R. and anticipated a nostalgic return to some of the places she had been with Anne Montignani. First, after checking in with Paris ARC headquarters, she would go to visit Mme. Coulet, her landlady when she and Anne had attended Sorbonne together. Paris had only been liberated for a month or so, and she wanted to present the older woman with some needed supplies. Before leaving she had gathered together various items the canteen could no longer use, just for that purpose.

In Ann's "Letters to Sara," she writes about that trip:

I found Mme. Coulet...and one of her old pensionnaires.... They told us of the hardship of living in a city during the occupation. Said they feared the cold more than hunger. Sometimes they would go to a movie theater just to sit with hundreds of other bodies in an effort to keep warm.

In Mme. Coulet's apartment was a little iron wood-burning or perhaps coal stove. They had enough fuel to light it for a couple of hours on Wednesday nights. So Wednesdays friends would come to their house. Other nights they would go to someone else's place.... Sascha, a French soldier, had gone off to war.... I saw him also, he had been a prisoner of war. When he put a glass down on a table and his mother rebuked him for leaving a ring, he said that it was "plus tranquille en prison."

I went to "Peggy Sage" where we [she and Anne M.] used to go for manicures...[and] bought a pair of wood and straw woven yellow and red shoes. Made my legs look great. They were the forerunners of platform shoes found in the USA about 10 years later.

Here are Ann Little's diary entries on the days she was in Paris:

> September 27: Sad is the day. I know he would come if he could and at this very instant he is miserable because he knows I am waiting for him.

> September 28: I departed via metro for lunch with Mme. Coulet. She looks very very different, very thin and shaky with a little monkey face. [Later] I was sitting on the terrace, just about to retire to my room when Mike suddenly appeared. He had been planning to sneak up on me...I think I saw him first.

After a heated interlude in an inelegant hotel room, Mike had immediately started in on his three favorite topics – the officers, the Red Cross Girls, and now France. Ann didn't find his harsh quips as funny as she once had and he insisted on disparaging her favorite city and second home. He didn't smell right to her either, not familiar, not like one of her kith and kin. Moreover his romancing had been proprietary and rough. She felt used and brittle. He was acting grabby and uncouth. Everything was so wrong that when he reached for her, she shrank back, leaving him pawing at the air.

The next morning she had a case of dry-mouth. She needed water. She longed for a deep hot bath. Her weeks of being attended by the chivalrous Colonel "Doc" Williams had made her feel valuable, interesting, redeemed. Michael Regond hadn't changed, he was the same person, but she was seeing him from a new remove and thinking of his hands on her suddenly made her skin crawl. Evidently their moment had passed. She hoisted up her chastity belt and buckled it firmly back in place. It was time to do a makeover and she was determined to channel a bit of Aunt Topsy and learn how to better "hold herself dear."

Ann writes about her next move in "Letters to Sara":

> While in Paris a call came from HQ to tell me that I was to be transferred to a fighter group.

> "Who is the Commanding Officer?"

> "Colonel Tipton."

> "That's nice, because I know him."

> So off I went to Vitry-le-François.

Chapter 26

FRANCE IN THREE-PART HARMONY

In Jim Tipton's "Oral History" (p. 53) he talks about what he did at headquarters before assuming his next command, the 358th:

> I went to the 19th TAC, and there I was. The only thing I remember doing there was that I finally located a Luftwaffe storehouse, which was full of champagne and cognac and got truckloads of it and took it back to base, and everybody was shaving with the finest champagne of the whole of France.

The bottle of champagne he brought to Ann, when she gave him the note for E.M.R., was from that stash. He had wanted to share his most excellent news about being assigned to lead a Thunderbolt group as opposed to mouldering on his backside at TAC headquarters. And though he recognized Ann Little as someone who would understand how important the new command was to him, he refrained. Jeannie would tell her soon enough. What he really wanted to do was goad her, just a touch, by mentioning those pies on Mike's cot.

Jim Tipton's style of command didn't allow him many people he could count on and Miss Little had earned his grudging respect. She was a resourceful and capable ARC director, even if she did get a little horsey at times. The two had been through a lot together. Besides, she always made him laugh, even when he tattled about pies. He still couldn't understand what she saw in Sergeant Regond.

In his memoir Jim writes about his interactions with subordinates as well as his personal vision of leadership, which I paraphrase here:

> One of my memories at Staplehurst is being cornered…by…a Red Cross Girl…and lectured about why I should "let my hair down" and become "one of the boys." She might as well have asked me to paint a Sistine Chapel ceiling. I was and am, more or less, a loner – don't mind it, rather enjoy it in fact, unless it becomes an issue.

> A little explanation of philosophy here. Any outfit needs ideals of integrity, dedication and perfection to cement loyalty into unity. Words. Words which are meaningless except when everybody

uses them every day. The key is "perfection" because there is no such thing and striving for the best, taking care of each little part, lets the whole enterprise happen.

It is a comfortable philosophy because one doesn't need to be a genius to live with it; each person working towards the same objective, getting better at doing the job and being given the wherewithal to do it. Loyalty coming from the top down as well as from the bottom up. Then there is the judgment factor, very imprecise, of understanding each particular individual's potential relative to their inherent capacity to produce the desired outcome; then getting rid of slackers and misfits.

In his "Oral History" (p. 90), Jim relates a conversation he had during his early days in the Army Air Corps:

> Man: "If I could have Hitler's power for one day, I would be happy to end my life. That would be the ultimate."
>
> Tipton: "You're kidding."
>
> Man: "No, just think of it. He has absolute power! Think of it – ABSOLUTE POWER!"
>
> Tipton: "Good Lord. Who wants that? It's ridiculous! What would you do with it? What good is it?"
>
> I was astounded. This was a learning experience for me. I thought I knew this chap. He wasn't much older than I; he was my boss, but in those days we were getting promoted so doggoned fast and were building up like mad. But that actually occurred, and I've never forgotten it.... I couldn't believe it. Obviously, people are like that, but that was my first experience with it.

After taking command of the 358th Thunderbolt tactical unit in France, Jim Tipton was in a mood. The Allies had achieved air superiority, mainly due to Patton's ground war, but Jim still wanted to be an Ace. With only two confirmed kills, he needed more engagement. The group was stymied in its hierarchical structure and he wanted to loosen things up, build a fire under the men and turn them into a "hot" unit.

One of the first things he did was go to Wing Command and ask if he could switch out some people at the top, give their slots to men who hadn't seen much action. He wanted to pull from replacements newly activated to join the unit, many with higher ranks and better training than "the next in line." He remembered how giddy he had felt the first time he got to fly combat. He wanted to give everyone a chance at that.

In his "Oral History" (p. 44-45), Jim describes the first of his three scariest moments in WW2; it happened when he went to ask for the authority to leverage the positions of the soldiers in his new unit:

When I first got to the 358th in the early stages, we were on an airbase on the Marne River.... Gen. "Tex" Sanders was my wing commander. He had his headquarters in his tent somewhere out in the boonies. I decided I had to go talk to him. I couldn't do it on the telephone because what I wanted to talk about was a little bit more confidential than could be exposed.... We had one of those L-5s [aircraft] on the base. A chap who was one of the controllers was using it.

Tipton: "Can I use it? I'd like to go over there."

Controller: "Sure. I'll check you out in it."

Tipton: "Check me out in it! Don't be silly. I know how to fly!!"

Controller: "Well, you don't want me to?"

Tipton: "Forget it!"

I dashed over there, got in the airplane, turned it on, taxied out, headed it down the runway and gave it throttle. When I got above those trees, that wind hit me. That darned airplane started going every which-a-way. I had never flown in a light airplane like that before. I was over-controlling; I couldn't keep the thing straight; I couldn't even make a turn. Thank God I was going in the right direction. If it had been going over enemy territory, I'd have been a captive.

It was a gusty, very heady day; a lot of eddies coming off those trees, and there I was. It scared me to death. That's the most frightened I've ever been in the war, believe it or not. In an L-5 twenty feet off the ground. I finally found myself where the wing headquarters was. I set it down in the field and walked over.

Tipton: "Here. You can have this doggoned thing."

I borrowed a car and went back to base. I never flew one again. (laughter) Well, anyway, that was a funny one.

Within a week of Colonel Tipton joining the 358th, they were relocated to Vitry-le-François, France, and a month later Ann Little was reassigned to his group and flew in from Paris as the Club Director with her new assistant Annette Roberts. Once again, as soon as she touched down, she found the commander and announced, "I am your new Red Cross Girl!" Colonel Tipton didn't look as surprised this time, though he did give her a curious look. It had been just nine days since she had last seen Mike.

In her diary Ann wrote:

October 7-8: It was with misgiving that I took over my new job. The situation was a difficult one indeed from the point of view of personalities. The club canteen was a shock and a disappointment to me. One lousy electric light bulb lit up a tent piled high with flour-sacks, tins, boxes, stoves, etc.

The boys cued up outside in the rain and mud and ate donuts outside in the dark. The john was a canvas partitioned off affair, sans roof. Our own tent was a complete mess of clothing, junk, etc. I put my bed behind a table and tried to take up as little room as possible. Sunday I went to chapel, which is held in our movie tent. The benches were all helter-skelter, tables piled up all over, the screen still up. Singing familiar hymns ["Rock of Ages," "Onward Christian Soldiers," and similar old standards] almost made me weep right in the middle of everything.

October 9: This day I started the cleaning up process. I arranged the lounge with flowers, books, etc. etc. Also tried to do something to the canteen. The movie tent still looks most unattractive, but at least it is neat. Patsy [the ARC director she was replacing] took all day and then some to straighten out the books. But, by nightfall all was in order and she is leaving in the morning.

October 11: There was a party at the Officers Club tonight and Annette and I were invited to attend. Some French gals were there and I was expected to act as hostess. This I willingly did, but the party was so terribly sticky that I turned from brandy to champagne to whiskey back to brandy. Anyway, I did a good job of mixing the people up and in the end everyone had a fine time.

October 12: On this day I could not raise my head off the pillow. I tried twice and failed miserably. Miss Annette very kindly took my morning shift for me....

October 13: Annette and I had a friendly chat with the Colonel to see just what could be done about our fast fading Aero Club. It seems to be getting away from us. It was finally decided, in the presence of all the executive officers, to move the entire business to a new site. We are to have heat, light, music and food. I wonder.

October 14: Our detail of 30 men appeared, under the command of Lt. Lazio, to move only the kitchen tent and to make floors for us. I worked hard and tried to keep the boys in coffee. My only thanks was to be called "The Whip" and to be told that our efforts were futile because we would be moving shortly.

October 15: Church looked much better this Sunday. I had flowers for the altar which seemed to make quite a difference.

October 16: This damp and dismal day was consumed by book-keeping. Imagine my surprise when, after hours of work, I hit the [canteen budget] nail on the head.

As promised, the unit did move again; they had only stayed in their miserable "tent city" for three weeks and three days. The new location was a reprieve from the mud and rain. There is a brief mention of it in Ann's "Letters to Sara":

We all went to Mormoulon-le-Grand. This was an erstwhile permanent French post. Annette and I had a room on the second floor of the Officers Club. We were warm, well fed, and perfectly comfortable. Annette was one who had been a school teacher. She knew everyone's name and what their job was. She seemed to be able to picture the whole military system and knew whom to ask for what. Wonderful.

As a part of the 358th, Ann was now required to view Colonel Tipton as a "real" boss. She didn't count the week before he handed over the 363rd and his Diablo Mustang to Reconnaissance, or when he was Colonel Meyer's deputy with the 366th. But in some ways she felt as if she was on somewhat equal footing with him. She was in charge of her ARC staff, just as he was in charge of his Air Corps troops, and by this time they knew each other — in every way except well. Many of their first impressions still lingered. She was pretty sure he would be considered a rube by her New York crowd, and he was just as sure his father could knock her off her high horse...cut her down to size.

The comfortable setup in Mormoulon-le-Grand began to foster a tenuous bond between Ann Little and Jim Tipton, as they played their parts in the arcane, predetermined order of things. It was understood that the lead man in an outfit should be seen enjoying the company of their assigned Red Cross girls, a position the troops both envied and expected. Without Mike around, Jim decided to press this advantage and make himself more known to the incomprehensible Miss Ann Little. Her ambivalence towards him was intriguing.

At breakfast in the mess hall Jim spoke of how he missed his mother's biscuits, which led Ann to reminisce about her father's tender poems and Alouette. In the canteen he'd describe his brother's superior memory and she'd counter with her sister's limitless creativity. Over drinks in the Officers Club she mentioned her old house in Rochester, its colorful past and scary rodents, giving him an excuse to ramble on about tracking animals in the timeworn Ozark Mountains, finding pawprints circling around deep chilly springs.

These blue watering holes were the jewels of his backwoods boyhood, flowing up and boiling out at the base of tall mossy cliffs, his secret discoveries in the sunken hollows of Missouri. In small exchanges, by telling her about the things that moved him, Jim was creating the rapport he wanted with the inscrutable Ann Little. Conversation came hard for him unless it was on a subject he was passionate about. She was a worthy listener.

Ann had noticed when Colonel Tipton began looking at her on the slant, but she wasn't open to another broken heart and didn't encourage him. She was determined to keep things on the up and up. It was late fall and Ann confides her misgivings about the Colonel's intentions in her diary:

November 4: Thoughts upon entering my fourth decade. I feel as young and playful as an innocent kitten. In the evening the Colonel gave me a lovely dinner party. Present were Colonel Beutnick, Captain Buchman, Captain Lisbee and Captain Hachlin, together with Annette and myself. I started out with two highballs and continued on until 3 in the morning with champagne. The party broke up and I piled into bed somehow – had a very odd invitation.

November 5: In the morning Ed, Ed and Sam brought breakfast up to me on a tray. I spent the day at the club feeling very ineffective. In the evening the stoves refused to work properly, the lights went out, etc. etc. After returning quite early and getting in about five hours of sleep I was awakened. There followed a long and fervent argument, which I finally lost. In so doing have possibly lost all. Anyway, the final words were most satisfactory....

November 6: Spent the day in preparation for our dance. Fran Park and Anne Luciane turned up. They are to be attached to the airborne outfit here. So we had 4 Red Cross girls and fourteen WACS at our dance. The music was very good. The Colonel came in which pleased the EMs [enlisted men]. They particularly enjoyed having Corporal Myer cut him after he had taken about three steps with me!

November 7: This day was spent in packing up to leave. I worked very hard piling up tables, packing games etc. etc. ... I am living my life over again. JBT [James Baird Tipton] is so much like [Mike?] in looks attitude and his feeling for me – whatever that is – that it really hurts. I wish to the highest power that I might have learned from my past experience. I do so wonder what it is I lack? Please someone "HELP!"

November 8: Guess I have not learned a blasted thing... In the evening I had a strange time and ended up by having my heart change my mind. It was not exactly satisfactory and the proper words were not forthcoming. I must say, though, that I did enjoy a late conversation.

That night Ann and Jim had dealt out bridge hands, face up, on top of her burlap covered "coffee table." They often played pairs, with the usual mediocre result as partners, so they were sitting, heads together, idly trying to fathom each other's bidding. The camp was moving again, and after a day of organizing equipment for departure, they both needed a little relaxation. Talking through bid responses seemed a perfect way to wind down. When Ann got prickly with him on some strategy he was trying to use, Jim attempted to justify himself, drawling out a "Now, Miss Annie...." Calling her, not the usual "Ann" or "Miss Little," but a disarming "Miss Annie," instantly closed the distance between them. She turned her head to his and leaned in to quietly ask, "Are you flirting with me?"

The double-beat Jim's heart took made him chuckle. He knew the answer. It was she that was flirting with him. Miss Little had let her guard down, shedding her "all or nothing" manifesto. For fair, she was only giving the enigmatic Colonel Tipton a single shot. But Jim felt Fate double back around and find him. Without overthinking it, he answered her question with their first real kiss. Startled, she kept her eyes open.

In the day-to-day, a little-along way of things a flare went up between Ann and Jim. They went beyond the glib back and forth of getting things done. Even when he was the commander's acting deputy in England, she had trusted his can-do engineering in many of the workables surrounding her life. For his part, he had grown to rely on her straightforward assessments of the pressures he sensed within his ranks. An observant listener, she noted a twist of the shoulders, clenched fists, crossed arms and restless eyebrows as conversational subtext. The enlisted men largely considered her their personal confidant and had shared many of their misgivings over that burlap-covered trunk. Jim was handy where Ann was savvy and vice versa. They were bound to make a good team.

Jim Tipton and Ann Little in Toul, France

Chapter 27

COMING IN FOR THE KILL

The Allies had Hitler on the defensive and ending the war seemed attainable, though it was far from a done deal. The 358th got stoked by Colonel Jim Tipton's intensity. If he wasn't exactly warm, he was fair and they admired that.

In December, 1945, a large, handsome, hardbound book titled *Orange Tails* was published "by and for the 358th Fighter Group and Ancillary Units." In his Foreword Brigadier General Glenn O. Barcus wrote of the group's commander, "Colonel James Tipton [was] a perfectionist who inspired and led the organization to the greatest possible achievements." A later passage in the book sums up his men's feelings toward him (p. 100):

> The Colonel's arrival caused the usual amount of griping, [but] the attitude soon changed to one of respect. As one GI put it, "That officer makes me work my fool head off, but I'd do anything for him!"

He got permission for the men to paint the tails of their fighter planes a bright orange, "so they can see who's coming." When there was time, he would go down to the airstrip and ask if any of his men wanted to go "Hun hunting" with him. These were not missions from HQ, but

Jim and his Thunderbolt P-47 crew, with the 358th Fighter Group; his nickname for me was "Miss Lass."

more of a spontaneous fly-about. He was their commander, but it was up to the men if they wanted to opt in. His passion to be an Ace was contagious and he loved the sky.

The "Orange Tails" outfit was in the process of leapfrogging across France. The resilient Thunderbolt P-47s were being utilized as tactical weapons on the front line and Colonel Tipton volunteered the 358th for every difficult mission Command could devise. "What the Hell" became his signature byline as they were moved from Mourmelon to Toul. They were racing along with the bombers and infantrymen in the ETO as the Allies forced their way through France. They bore down on the Nazis, pushing them back. By then tales of the experimental German rocket planes and suicidal Japanese pilots had blackmailed their minds, extorting from them whatever it took to prevail.

On November 9th, 1944, the 358th unit followed in Patton's wake, the women of the ARC in tow. The wet frigid weather sent Ann and Annette scurrying to find warm, dry lodging. They dickered for a small home by offering to pay rent with their combined allotment of coal. It was situated on the edge of the airfield, a short walk down a country road to their canteen.

Years later, in Alabama in the 1960s, Ann gave a speech about her experiences in WW2 where she describes their accommodations in Toul:

The house belonged to Mademoiselle and Monsieur Thouvenot, whose daughter Charlotte lived with them. Mademoiselle Charlotte was the one to open the door when we went to inquire. She did not seem to be the maid, nor yet the mistress of the house, although she answered the door with a towel around her head and a broom in her hand. This house had been a billet for a senior German officer during the occupation, so the family was used to putting up with invaders of one sort or another. We learned that Charlotte was their 25-year-old "unmarried" daughter and as such was expected to do their housework. One evening we heard her singing in the basement. She was tending three little goats! The house was so clean that we had lived there two weeks without knowing there were goats in the house! She used to wash her cat in the kitchen sink and put him in the back of the oven with the door open all wrapped up in a towel to keep him warm. We liked her very much. We offered Mademoiselle Charlotte a job as cashier at the club and her mother wouldn't permit her to work there. Afraid she might meet some terrible American and marry him.

Here are some of Ann's most telling diary entries during her first month with the Thouvenots:

November 14: Could it be that today is my birthday? [no, her birthday was November 4] Here follows a list of presents he has bestowed upon me today – cigarette ration, picture, 2 eggs, 1 bottle brandy, 1 bottle Benedictine, tooth powder, 1 bottle perfume. Previously it was playing cards, a belt to hold my pants up, champagne, vitamin pills. I don't know....

November 24: This day I had a bath in the new quarters of the HQ offices. The house is built smack up to a lumber factory where Papa Mathew [a German sympathizer ousted by Patton] made his fortune. The house is a gawdawful French idea of Hollywood. Hideous tiled hall and modernistic stain glass entrance, complete with fountain, greet the eye upon entering. I think the salon and dining room are not too bad.... The life-sized photographs of the daughter [Papa Mathew's?] taking her first communion over the Colonel's bed about got me.

The "Wheel House," where the "big wheel" officers of the 358th
lived in Toul

November 26: This afternoon the officers threw a party at the mansion. T'was just like an old-fashioned cocktail party at home with people spending an entire afternoon in light banter. Highlight – The Colonel posing on top of the mantelpiece. I was playing games with him like a silly girl. My forte is not coquetry and I should know better – at any rate it all straightened itself out as anything that is real should. By now I am in a fine state of dithers.

November 28: In the evening the tall one and I did my book-keeping – it was off and annoyed me no end. The sitting room of their abode looks so much like a hotel lobby that I kept expecting people to come in with their luggage. Highlight of the evening was when Jimmie called Sammy by ringing the doorbell with his foot. We were all giggles and explanations.

When General Patton and his ground army first came through Toul, the town's mayor, Monsieur Schmidt, asked the general how he might help. Patton suggested that he encourage young women to attend the ARC Saturday night dances. This was not a simple request. During times of war it was customary for the French to refrain from outward displays of gaiety, considering it "dancing on the cadavers of fallen heroes." "Old blood and guts" Patton explained that these gatherings boosted morale, that "Eat, drink and be merry, for tomorrow we die" was the embodiment of the American warrior's philosophy.

Thanks to Patton, the townspeople were uncommonly gracious to the Orange Tails and allowed 100 of their daughters, along with 10 hand-picked chaperones to jitterbug with the Yankees. Ann was where she could do the most good, conversing with the mayor and his elegant wife in their native tongue, organizing live music, giving the town's children rare treats and teaching French to the soldiers, who were suddenly more inclined to learn the language of the country they occupied.

In her "Letters to Sara," Ann writes about the first dance in Toul:

We had Christmas trees in the corners of the large room and good music, albeit canned. The bar offered coffee and doughnuts. The chaperones, who had not had coffee in five years, practically prevented anyone else from getting near the place! They asked what we did with the grounds! Can you imagine the leading ladies of a small town asking their hostess what she did with the garbage? Believe me, after that we emptied the coffee grounds in one special container, the lard (for cooking doughnuts) in another. We never asked who picked the stuff up. As for Mademoiselle Schmidt, she was elegantly dressed in a black wool dress, had a little black velvet bow in her stylishly done up auburn hair, and on her feet guess what? The high-top black shoes off her fancy skates. The party was really fun. For once a planned affair had all the spontaneity of a spur-of-the-moment party.

One boy said to me, "Where did you find these girls? I've never seen any of them before." I explained he wouldn't have, they were not allowed out on the streets. It was very nice because later on many of them were invited into French homes for Sunday dinner and so on. One time a boy asked me if there was anyone who spoke Polish. The mayor's wife did and they were introduced. They began jabbering at once. I never knew of any romances, but I'm sure there were some.

But alas, just as the party was in full swing, along came Jerry. An air-raid. From fun and frolic to abject fear in one moment. I didn't know whether or not to turn off all the lights with all these young boys and girls buttoned up together, the chaperones were so shaken they were no help. It was all over in a few minutes, and everyone went home.

After that, they said they would not attend any dances at the field, as it was "too much the target." We had to agree and planned the next dance to be held at the theater in town, which had been closed up lo these many years. We got an allotment of coal, the furnaces were lit, we hired the 82nd Airbourne band, we had cookies and lemonade made up and Ann Little was standing over a register letting warm air go up her skirt. Wonderful.

Comes a telephone call. 82nd cannot come. It was already Saturday afternoon. How to set up some canned music quickly? Another call. 'Twere the executive officer to say Colonel Tipton had canceled the party. Why? Battle of the Bulge was on.

In his "Oral History" (p. 71-72) Jim talks about the final German offensive in WW2. It became known as the Battle of the Bulge and took place from December 16, 1944, through January 25, 1945. The evening he first heard about the Germans massing their troops in the Ardennes region of Belgium for a showdown included an incident he would later describe as the second most frightened he had ever been in the war:

We had two Red Cross Girls with us, one of whom I married later after the war was over; Ann Little, her name was. The Wheel House, they called it, was a rather nice civilian home, which the French had confiscated from some people who had been supporting the Germans during their occupation, and turned it over to the military. This was the home for me and my staff.

That particular evening – which was during the early part of the Bulge with bad weather; keep in mind we had all of these alerts for these saboteurs who would drop in on us at any time – we were sitting in the dining room playing bridge. The two Red Cross Girls were our guests that evening. I was playing opposite Ann, and my adjunct was playing with the other girl, and we were bidding at this particular point.

My wife was sitting in the corner of the room, I was facing her. I was watching her because she was getting ready to make her bid. She looked beyond my shoulder, and her eyes became very wide, and she let out this horrible scream. The back of my hair stood up! I knew dad-burned well the whole German Army was there behind us.

It was a mouse! I've never gotten over that or let her forget it, incidentally. But that was a horrifying thing.

In Ann's diary entry about that same evening, she wrote:

In the most serious moment of bridge I saw a mouse and crawled up on a chair in true Blondie [comic-strip] style. The shriek I emitted practically made my flak-weary, combat-fatigued Colonel faint. Maj. Hall declared he didn't know I had it in me and Capt. Benjamin said he'd seen everything. The three of them killed Mr. Mouse and took him into the kitchen. The three girls out there screamed likewise. It's international I guess.

Continuing with Jim's description of that night, the beginning of Hitler's last stand:

We were alerted to expect any kind of activity: sabotage, air troop drops – paratrooper types, anything. We were on a tremendous amount of alert and rather on edge because we couldn't fly. The weather was hanging in.

I do remember one request that came in from the Army: "Could you somehow get into the Valley of the Rhine down there?" They gave the location. "We think there is something happening; we aren't quite sure." So the operations officer, Joe Tyler, called me up and told me about the request.

I said, "Nobody but a damned fool would fly in this kind of weather. Set me up an aircraft, and I'll go do it." He said "Okay." I didn't know how I was going to do it, but at least I wasn't going to <u>ask</u> anybody to do it. About 15 minutes later, before I got my stuff together...he called up and said, "Colonel. Don't worry. We've gotten lots of volunteers; you don't have to go." It made me proud of the unit to do something like that.

Here are a few excerpts relating to the Battle of the Bulge from *Orange Tails* (p. 91-92, 98, 107):

In a way, the Germans benefited from the loss of France and Belgium. The Allies now found their armies at the far end of the long and tenuous supply lines. German soldiers on the other hand stood in prepared positions, practically on their own border. An excellent network of roads and railways connected them with their factories...they could fight back, they <u>would</u> fight back. Patton's tanks had outrun their supplies. As winter began to drape over the European landscape, it became increasingly clear that the period of fluid operation was over.

Because of the work done during the period of the German breakthrough, and specifically January 1st, the Group was awarded their second Distinguished Unit Citation.... From 24 December, 1944 to 2 January 1945, the 358th Fighter Group...[was] principally responsible for the maintenance of air superiority against a resurgent German Air Force.

In several quotes from his "Oral History" (p. 65-77), Jim responds to questions about the Battle of the Bulge and labels it as one of many miscalculations on Hitler's part. At the time the Germans had only one army available, just an armored division, to use as a spearhead against four Allied armies spread along the Rhine. Their only real advantage was the bad weather, which had grounded the Allied air forces. "They [the German army] could do this type of thing when we couldn't use our air," my father commented. As far as he was concerned the war had been won, and yet this last offensive by the Nazis represents one of the bloodiest fights of the entire conflict.

Jim Tipton thought the answer "Nuts!" was an appropriate response by General McAuliffe to the German Commander who had asked him to surrender at Bastogne on December 22, 1944, during the Bulge. The media made that "Nuts" answer out to be "big news," but Jim thought maybe the losing German strategy explained the offhand remark, since when the sky cleared and there were "nice crisp winter days with sun," the obvious happened. Allied air and ground forces ultimately prevailed and the Nazi fighters began their final retreat. But the "inevitable" only occurred after there were horrific casualties on both sides. Tipton then speculated that the real purpose of the doomed attack may have been to broker a better deal.

> What could they do? Who knows? Probably just trying to save time, perhaps to make a better surrender under terms which would be more advantageous to the Germans. I haven't any idea why. Then, of course, the Germans' front was still going on and they were being completely subjugated. Amazing things those Germans did, when you think how close they came.

In Jim's "Oral History" he talks about other lapses in Hitler's reasoning, especially when the Third Reich had failed to develop their most innovative armaments (p. 60-63):

> They didn't have a lot [of rocket planes]. The whole point I'm making is that these were experimental. The smart air people in Germany wanted to go these routes, and Hitler didn't have an advanced concept enough to permit them to do so. It might have changed their whole aspect of the war if the Luftwaffe had gone the way they [the German generals] had wanted to go.... Don't forget also that one of the things we were hitting over there were [secret] targets – we had a code name for it [Heavy Water]....

> If Hitler had been a little more astute and not so anxious and greedy and delayed a few things, he might have been able to develop something we would never be able to resist.

Chapter 28

TAKING THE NEXT STEP

Soon after the initial kiss, Ann felt compelled to tell her friend Jeannie about the recent developments. She wanted to write to her, wanted Jeannie to be the first to know how her feelings had changed for the Colonel, how their relationship had deepened. She was hesitant about sending a message out too soon, but contrary to her original intuition, the romance had taken hold. Things moved fast in the European Theater of Operations during WW2. She eventually put aside her skepticism and got a note off, but Jeannie never wrote her back. From Ann Little's "Letters to Sara":

> In the winter one day Jimmie heard that Jeannie was sick and recuperating in the south of France. He said "Let's call her and ask her to come visit." Of course I had to agree, although in my heart I wondered how in the world such a visit would turn out. In my little office he put through a telephone call on a field telephone. This was a type of gadget that one had to holler into and shout code names for the next station. Finally he was able to reach her and, after much shouting back and forth, he made her understand that he wanted her to come visit. I never spoke with her and I guess he did not identify himself very well because she never showed up. Later I heard that she had gone to visit the airfield of her brother! She thought it was he who had called.

The 1st of April Miss Annie and Jimmie were relocated to occupied Germany. As recounted in the *Orange Tails* (p. 129):

> This move would be different from the others. We were going into hostile territory, and security would be far more important than ever before.

> As the convoy left the friendly town of Toul, the men wondered if they'd ever be back again to renew friendships made there. French farmers were up early, and paused in their work to wave to the Yanks.

> It wasn't long, though, before the road signs changed from French to German, and the people reflected sullen hate and

fear.... The destruction that greeted the eyes of everybody on those convoys took them completely by surprise. Wrecked towns and destroyed buildings were in evidence all across France, but here in Germany was destruction on a scale undreamed of before...along the roads German civilians pushing carts with non-descript household articles would occasionally stumble dangerously into the path of the trucks. They were on their way back. "Back to what?" was the question.

Colonel Tipton got hit over Germany, his third deathly fright. He explains the circumstances in his "Oral History" (p. 79):

I went over there [to Sandhofen] one day, just to get the lay of the land because, being the boss, I had to go get the best operational situation I could, including the best quarters for me, perhaps. In any case, I was laying the thing out, and went back to Toul.

The next day something happened, and for some reason I decided to go back again. Just the engineers were there and the army, the rear echelon, really. Of course, they had the air defense set up.... I figured they would recognize me.... When I arrived over the airbase, all hell broke loose, the whole artillery. Only one man needs to shoot, and this is license for everyone to shoot... well this is what happened to me in this little AT-6.

Anyway, they started shooting. Fortunately, they didn't start firing until I was sort of making my initial approach, so I was rather low, about 1000 feet. When they did that, I just dumped over and got it right on the deck and stayed down there, hedge-hopping, and kind of snuck in on them and stuck it down on the runway, which was still full of bomb holes and hadn't really been repaired, but you don't need much runway for an AT-6; it's a training aircraft.

I'm madder than hell. Incidentally, I had my executive officer [with me], who was Lt. Col. Therriault. He was white as a sheet. Of course I had been active trying to dodge those knockers, and I was just mad, madder than blazes. We swung around and parked the aircraft...this captain of artillery, who was commander of this unit, came up to the aircraft. I was unbuckling and opened the canopy and looked down at him...his face was literally ashen. I looked at him, and his face – I just burst out laughing – I couldn't say a word! He was just so horrified! ... I never did get a chance to cuss out the antiaircraft people, I got so tickled at the commander. Of course that horrified him even more, I guess, when I was laughing at his unit...they hit the plane. Just a light round, though. They didn't hit me with that explosive stuff.

Before going to the Sandhofen district of Manheim, the 358th had been well settled in Toul for five months and my mother was worried about abandoning her French kitchen staff, a disabled man and wife, with their daughter, plus another woman and her daughter. The five of them would be left with no support and France was in ruins. Ann showed Jimmie another side of herself by ignoring protocol. She bundled up her work crew – right along with the rest of her ARC supplies – and put them in the back of her supply truck. She was riding shotgun up front and each time there was a stop she heard her French refugees behind her shouting "Camouflage, camouflage!" before throwing army blankets over their heads. At the checkpoints, when the military guards looked in, they saw nothing but "equipment" and waved them on. Recently occupied by the Allies, their destination of Sandhofen was formerly a Luftwaffe airbase, which included the site of an abandoned Nazi concentration camp.

In Ann's "Letters to Sara," she recounts what she and her assistant found at their new German post:

> Annette and I were in the basement someplace in a whitewashed room and on the wall was painted "ACHTUNG" and a lot more stuff. I think it had something to do with the plumbing... there was one huge shower and bathroom place with all the toilets stopped up. It was an awfully smelly mess. I think left by our American men who had but recently "liberated" the place. I was feeling sorry for myself thinking that I didn't see any reason why a nice girl such as I was supposed to clean up after a bunch of no good infantrymen.

There would be no way my mother could have known she was cleaning up a gas-chamber in that eerie below ground room. If my father suspected the truth, he wouldn't have disabused her of considering the space a "dormitory-style bathroom for servicemen," recognizing the stark implications.

In his "Oral History" (p. 77-78), Jim talks about the war's end and his only firsthand knowledge about the gas showers used in the Nazi genocide:

> Oh, I think it just crept up on you because you could see the demise of German resistance, certainly. Don't forget, for a while

there, after we had gotten into our air base across the Rhine in Germany, they literally stopped our Army troops at the Elbe and sat there and waited. We weren't doing anything.

As a matter of fact, my flight surgeon, while we were there and before the war was over, made a trip to one of Hitler's camps. I've forgotten which one; one of those horrible camps where they were exterminating the Jews and so on. He came back, even though he was a pretty seasoned doctor, green around the gills at what he had seen there, and tried to describe it. It was just incomprehensible to anybody that could listen to it. We knew it was all substantiated; it was true.

In her "Letters to Sara," Ann sums up her first impression of being in occupied Germany this way:

We finally did get our canteen operating. Shortly after arrival, in comes Colonel T. looking for a cup of coffee and a doughnut. He runs his finger over the greasy rack (upon which to drain the doughnuts) and announced it was dusty. Naturally, after a ride in a truck. Did I honestly think, said I to myself, that I could be a wife to this white gloved inspector?

Strange how things work out. My parents fell in love despite themselves. Ann was still having reservations about this hard to read man, just as Jim was increasingly convinced he was about to die. Nevertheless, neither of them could imagine a life in the far off States, or basically anywhere, without the other. When Jimmie looked directly at her and said "Get your fanny out of this place. Get back home and wait for me there," she was thrilled. Not the proposal she had always dreamed of, but they had often shared similar doubts about wartime marriages – far too risky.

Jimmie made arrangements to fly her to Paris, where she needed to be granted permission for release. While there, enjoying just about the only real leave he had allowed himself, he bought a watercolor of the oldest bridge in the city, the Pont Neuf, which means "New Bridge" in French (I see the painting every day in my living room). Watching her handsome man negotiate -- "how much for the painting?" -- Miss Annie wished for three things, to be home, for him to follow and for the war to be over.

In 26 pages, torn from a cheap lined-paper notebook, my mother wrote a day-by-day travelogue about her departure from Europe and she titled it "By Ann Little, A Red Cross Gal on the Move." Here are some excerpts from that journal, her last dated writings from WW2:

On May 4th I received verbal permission to return home from [HQ in] Paris. On May 7th I received written confirmation of the permission and instructions to report to the Personnel Dept., "when the time came," i.e., when a replacement arrived. Since no one had come to relieve me as of May 25, I decided to go to Paris. [After arriving] I was told to come back on Monday, May 28, with all my luggage.

The plan was [for Jimmie and me] to fly to A55 [airstrip], Colonel "Doc" Williams's camp, where he was going to let us have a car for our use in Paris. The weather closed in and I became so nervous that I didn't dare look out of the plane.... He [Jim] seemed to be looking all over the sky. I couldn't tell whether he seemed anxious.... I thought he might be worried about me. We swooped down among the tree tops and telephone poles and came through a little opening and right onto an airfield. It was St. Dizier. When the motor died and all was quiet, I heard him say, "It's rough – rough."

So there we were, sort of cold and miserable and wet in the middle of France [delayed a day by the weather]. And I kept wondering if the gal [at headquarters] would be cross because I had not shown up on Monday as scheduled. I thought and said at the time that during the long lonely hours of traveling that lay ahead of me I would probably wish for that moment when we were marooned together to return. At the time we just didn't know how it would all turn out.

After supper the clouds broke and we took off again for A55. All went well. Colonel Williams came and fetched us and we sat about his room all evening. I stayed with the ARC girls. They lived in a cold sort of bombed out building and, tired as I was, I had difficulty in getting to sleep in that place.

Next morning I didn't see Jimmie at all. I drove into Paris.... When Jimmie arrived in the afternoon he was irked because his orders would not permit him into a good hotel. Jimmie and I were so tired that we had a rather punk evening and he left me to wait till Thursday for him to come back. I felt distinctly unhappy about the whole thing, thinking that things had gotten off to a very poor start.

Well, he came back Thursday, May 31st.... He had arranged for a nice room at the Ritz. Then I found out that all transportation for ARC personnel had been canceled by the Army and no promise of when the embargo would be lifted. We were still determined to have a good time. Even waiting two hours for lunch couldn't get us down, when we were left alone together.

Afterwards we went to the Rodin museum in the afternoon, and then did a bit of shopping till supper. Saturday afternoon we went to the Auteuil races and Jimmie lost.... On Sunday we really went sightseeing in earnest, from Sacre Coeur, to the Louvre, to Notre Dame, to the Luxembourg Gardens. We bought two books and some etchings. We went into a cute little bar next to my hotel and topped the evening off with a drink.

Monday Jimmie left me after lunch and I stood in the sun feeling very sorry for myself, then started over to my job in an ARC service club that was hectic and noisy and hot and very busy. I had to dance with drunks, talk with bores; it was like starting all over again. When Jimmie came back and saw the situation he insisted I be assigned to a job at HQ, and I wound up in a file room, a la Swiss Legation. It was very good work for the purpose and I moved to the Hotel de Malte.

On June 15, I was informed that I was to be among a group of girls going home, and I was to report for final clearance the next morning. I called Jimmie to let him know and he came the next day and was able to spend the weekend with me in Paris. We took a walk in the Tuileries Garden and sat on a bench making plans. He wanted a small, simple wedding. Saturday night we went to our little bar and just talked.

On Sunday we went to the Russian Cathedral. The music was really wonderful and of course Jimmie could see over everyone's head. When anything spectacular happened he'd lift me up to see! After lunch we spent the afternoon over by the Île de la Cité in order to take pictures of Jimmie's bridge.

In the evening we ate in the officers' mess and talked and planned some more. By this time I was in a little glow of happiness that I felt sure people must be able to see. The next day Jimmie and I took the bus out to the Vélizy-Villacoublay to say our fond fare-well. I felt sad and happy all alone....

On Tuesday I was informed that we were not to leave until Sat-urday! What I did to keep busy I don't know. Anyway, Friday I met Annette and that was a big help. She brought news of Jim-mie.

Finally, on June 23rd, we [ARC girls going home] left Paris. Upon arrival we were informed that they had never heard of us and would not put us on the next boat. Upon leaving, a brick fell off the roof and landed about two feet in front of me on the side-walk!

In an "all alone in an Italian Garden" moment Ann looked down at the brick, hugged her ribs tightly and dropped in a slump onto her footlocker. It was filled with a mess of dirty laun-dry, a half dozen bottles of French champagne for her wedding and three plundered spoils of war from Jimmie: a long Ger-man sword he had packed diagonally into her trunk, a red and black Nazi ban-ner that his men had giv-en him and an officer's Luger, which she had carefully wrapped in her burlap topper and buried down at the bottom of her erstwhile "coffee table," now hope chest.

She could hear her-self beginning to whimper, but there was no stopping the ache. Rocking, she began to keen and wail longer and louder than at any time during the last 16 months and didn't give a good god damn if anyone

Nazi flag seized by the 45th Infantry Division in the Nuremburg Stadium and sent by them to Jim Tipton (second from right) and his 358th outfit, the Orange Tails, with this advice, "Use it for engine rags or some other useful purpose."

saw or heard her, right there on the sidewalk next to the boarding dock. As she continues in her "Red Cross Gal on the Move":

> It [the brick] didn't hit me, so I don't know why I felt so upset about it. We [ARC girls] found billets in a very peculiar looking haunted house on a cliff. Show people, ARC, WACs, nurses, French women, etc....and that's the vacuum I'm in.

> Monday June 25. Went down to "Area 1" to see about "this here Sea Porpoise," and it is scheduled to leave Thursday June 28 – Lordee. Monday, Tuesday and Wednesday. We should board her along about Wednesday afternoon, so that means only two more nights in my flea infested bed.

Postcard from Ann to Aunt Topsy,
July 10, 1945

Friday July 6 – Whee! Today the S.S. Wakefield will dock at Boston Harbor and I'll be in Rochester tomorrow.

It had taken two months for Ann to get home after coming to Paris for that very purpose. In a postcard addressed simply to "Miss Alice O. Little, Cherry Valley, New York," she wrote:

Dear Aunt Topsy, I arrived home Sat. morning after docking in Boston Friday afternoon. Now I'm waiting for Jimmie – the Col. – to return too. He should arrive between the 20th & 30 of July. He is going home to Ark. & then coming here with his mother and father. I hope for [sic] to marry me. I'll let you know as soon as I can just what the date will be – With love from Ann.

Chapter 29

THE END OF THE WORLD AS WE KNOW IT

Jim Tipton wrote in his 1982 memoir:

One must stop and remember that the fighter group of that day – or any WW2 military unit for that matter – was not far from 99.6% pure civilian; a hodgepodge of people from anywhere in the U.S., hastily trained, short in experience, and nearly all personnel would return to a civilian province interrupted by the war.

By the summer of 1945 Colonel Tipton figured he'd "had it." He wasn't sleeping. He was frenetic and exhausted, believing in his heart that the next round, friend or foe, had his number on it. Even then, he was still aiming to be an Ace before he died. The goal gave him a reason to get out of bed and face the morning. In his many ground raids he had taken out another German plane that was confirmed, along with others that weren't, but he never got a fourth or fifth "victory." He longed for the opportunity of one more air-to-air score.

Jim Tipton with his three "victory" insignia painted on the side of his aircraft

Looking back on being a fighter pilot in WW2, he wrote this in his memoir:

> Magnificent overall, chaotic in detail. I watched it from three separate fighter groups flying out of more than ten airfields, hopping from England to France to Germany; all within a short eighteen month timeframe.... I'm eternally amazed.

VE day was May 8th, and the war was over on the European front.

Ann married Jim Tipton on August 4th, 1945, in an intimate ceremony on a bluff overlooking Lake Ontario.

On August 6th and 9th the United States dropped two atomic bombs on Japan. One on Hiroshima, then one over Nagasaki. The United States implemented the nuclear option, with the consent of the United Kingdom, and that decision changed everything for everyone.

Jim and his bride Ann, with her sister and bridesmaid Jane and her brother Bill's son Skip

THE MORGUE

THE MORGUE

Dr. Paul Light Tipton (PLT) died on October 9, 1971, at age 91, from a stroke. I was away at college at the time, and he was kept on life support until my grandmother gave their physician authority to stop all medical intervention. It was terrifically difficult for her to make the decision and it took him over three long, grim weeks to die. He was stubborn to the end.

Mrs. PLT, Hettie Newfield Baird (Tipton), died on May 4, 1989, at age 98, from late stage dementia.

Dr. Tipton, known to me as "Grande," looking much the same as I remember him.

Miss Hettie, known to me as "Momette," also as I remember her and a rare photograph where she is actually smiling, almost...

Colonel Richard Pike Tipton, died on March 26, 2011, at age 93, from renal failure. After dropping out of medical school, he had followed his big brother into a military career in the United States Air Force. He served as a 1st Lieutenant with the 321st Bombardment Group in the European-African-Middle Eastern Campaign flying B-25s in WW2. He christened his bomber "Miss Hettie's Pride and Joy," and he fondly remembered racing "liberated" motorcycles along abandoned airstrips at full throttle. He was obviously Miss Hettie's favorite, just as Jim had been Dr. Tipton's. Uncle Tip had too much of my grandfather in him to be the favored son.

Aunt Bettye Carla Borom (Tipton), Uncle Tip's wife, died on February 10, 1979, at age 50 from a cancer that started in her knee. She was much younger than Tip

"Tip," to most people, but known to me as "Uncle Dick," 2nd from right; he named his bomber after his mom.

and had kept him stewing for over a year before agreeing to marriage. In two years she bore him a boy, Rick, and then a girl, Pat. It was her 24-year-old daughter that willingly paused her life to come home and live beside her mother as she fought to stay alive. Aunt Bettye's grizzly impatience with any topic that involved death made it impossible for my cousin to comfort her or for my aunt to give peace to her family.

Tip and Bettye in 1962

Uncle Tip stunned everyone when, immediately after Aunt Bettye's death, he set out on a mission to visit four prospective mates. One of the possibilities was an ARC nurse that he had known intimately in the war. Supposedly she was still single because of him, but he only got as far as the top name on his list, choosing a woman that didn't get along with either of his children or any of us. She was his first cousin Nell, and she predeceased him too.

Dr. Lit, Seelye William Little, died on February 28, 1937, at age 70, after a series of strokes; the beginning signs may have been blood clots in his legs. He studied at Columbia University, published a book on nephritis, wrote many articles on cancer, was the Secretary of the

Medical Advisory Board during WW2 and later an examiner for the Federal Pension Board, along with being on Staff at Rochester's General Hospital and a physician for the city's Orphan Asylum.

Dr. Lit as a youth   *Mama Lit as a young woman*

Mama Lit, *Mary Bellows Dodds (Little)*, died in her sleep on October 17, 1948, at age 72, from unknown causes. On the day she died, she had been visiting her older daughter in nearby Pultneyville. After announcing she felt tired, she left Jane and Monty's home with her customary revved up engine hurling her out of their driveway by popping the clutch to get a good head start. She then drove off to Alouette in her pea-green, two door Ford sedan. She was a short person who could barely reach the pedals and managed to see the road ahead only by peering through the steering wheel.

Uncle Bill, William Seelye Little, died on June 20, 1976, at age 70, from inoperable pancreatic cancer. He had served stateside in WW2 in the Army Corps of Engineers and was awarded the Legion of

Uncle Bill and Aunt Sue as newlyweds

Merit for inventing the Shadow Compass, a desert navigational device used in the field. He was often tapped by the famous warrior, George Patton, for his wisdom on competitive sailing and celestial navigation — which was an honor, but also a duty that otherwise occupied him on what should have been his days off. He rose to Lt. Colonel in the ranks before returning to the civilian world.

Aunt Sue at age 25

Aunt Sue, Virginia Harriet Peck (Little), died on April 15, 1982, at age 68 of a breast cancer that eventually consumed her whole body. She was upstairs in her bedroom with a personal nurse and the younger of her two sons, Henry, when she passed. The elder son, Skip, could not be there. The home had been in her family for generations. 2762 Elmwood Avenue was formerly a tenant dwelling for the Peck Farm of Peck Apple fame, the only remnant to survive the Great Depression of her family's original settlement. That area is commonly known as 12 Corners, Brighton, New York.

Uncle Jim, James Bellows Little, died on Dec 19, 1988, at age 81, from a heart failure that occurred during the night at his in-town house. He was found the next morning, still in his bed, by his second wife, Cynthia. They kept the tradition of having separate bedrooms. He had managed to cheat death for a decade after surviving a massive heart attack and changed my mother's expectations by breaking through the 70-year

Aunt Bet and Uncle Jim as newlyweds

jinx that seemed, in her mind, to be the ultimate lifespan for all Littles.

Aunt Bet, Elizabeth Farley (Little), died on July 21,1998 at age 88, from "old age," apparently becoming more and more frail, spending her time playing solitaire, drinking an occasional toddy with a cigarette and enjoying her horses, until she passed away in her sleep. Her daugh-

Betty Farley

ter, Farley, also a skilled horsewoman, was sitting on the bed beside her. Her son Zeke could not be there.

Aunt Jane, Jane Chamberlin Little (Phillips/Goodwin), died on April 2, 1962, at age 52, from breast cancer. One of the treatments used with her disease had been developed by my grandfather and her father, Dr. Lit, many years before and was still in current practice at the time. Mother was very practical and kept many of Aunt Jane's clothes. I wore the coral colored, silky quilted shorty bed-robe she probably died in until it fell apart years later. My children no doubt remember it.

Aunt Jane and Uncle Monty as newlyweds

Uncle Monty, Montague Phillips, died on August 10, 1951 at age 47, from a fatal head injury. He was in the Virgin Islands, looking at investment properties, when he tripped over some uneven steps leading to a harbor and fell. Aunt Jane got the call about the accident from Uncle Jim right before he hopped a plane to St. Thomas to investigate the circumstances. She and her brother were both with him when he passed away in the hospital. Monty had served in the United States Army Air Corp during WW2.

Uncle Frank, Aunt Jane, Miss Annie and Jimmie (Sir) in Japan, 1960

Uncle Frank Goodwin married Aunt Jane a year later, knowing she was terminally ill. He was lucky. After Monty died Aunt Jane needed lawyers to help her with her estate and doctors to help her with her cancer and one of each proposed. There were other suitors as well, but she wisely chose Uncle Frank to become her second husband. He was her lawyer, this was his first marriage, and he became a most beloved addition and benefactor to the extended Little clan for many years.

Ann Livingston Little Tipton ("Miss Annie") died on August 10, 2004, at age 89, from liver cancer that had metastasized from her colon. She declined medical attention and entered hospice, was in no pain and still had her extraordinary mind when she died three months after being diagnosed. She was in her own bed, with her children and one of her only two grandchildren, along with my soon-to-be husband, seated nearby.

From her deathbed she could only listen as we watched a 20-year-old video of a younger Miss Annie sitting next to her Jimmie as she read aloud from a turquoise spiral notebook, regaling us with her early life in Rochester. My mother's long last exhale happened just as we were seeing her recorded-self begin to tell about her dog Toqué. My sister was holding my mother's hand and confirmed she was gone. None of us had seen that video before, as the filming had been a "trial run" for a new camcorder, shot by my father to learn how to use the camera's tripod remote control. I had brought it for "entertainment," randomly plucked from a pile of family tapes I had at home, thinking it might be a long night for all of us. At the time I had no idea she had written a memoir.

Toqué, my mother's childhood pet

James Baird Tipton ("Sir") died on March 29, 1994, at age 79, from prostate cancer, a disease that took 11 years to kill him. "Sir," his nickname of nearly half a century, was diagnosed and operated on in 1983, but I think he had already known something was wrong. His 1982 handwritten memoir has an "of the moment" intensity about it that makes me feel sure he was already then grappling with his own mortality.

He died in a rented hospital bed that he and Miss Annie had set up in the living room of their Florida home. It looked out over Lake Clay, which is known for its almost daily rainbows. They had been living in Alabama and had just put down earnest money on the lake place when the doctors verified his sickness, so when he got out of his initial treatment, they packed up their Montgomery home of 20 years and Miss Annie took care of Sir in Florida, feeding him avocado and grapefruit from the trees in their backyard to keep him healthy. His decline was gradual and they had over a decade more together, but they both knew it was done by the evening of March 28th.

That night Ann sat next to him and watched the sun set over the water through the triple sliding-glass doors. There were no rainbows. She stayed with him, talking about everything that mattered, until early morning. Exhausted, she went to rest on the couch beside him and within a few moments she heard him sigh. He had found his opening and took off.

I got the call at four in the morning of the 29th and drove the 11-hour trip from North Georgia to Highlands County, Florida, to be with Miss Annie. By the time I arrived she had developed red spots on her forearms and legs. Within a month the palms of her hands were raw, the soles of her feet were peeling off and all of her hair had fallen out. The doctors said it was psoriasis. After about a year her skin had cleared up, but her salt and pepper hair came back pure white.

On the Thanksgiving after my mother died, in 2004, my family had a final ceremony for "Sir and Miss Annie." Dr. Tipton's, Miss Hettie's and Sir's ashes were all in Lake Martin, Alabama. When my sister and I poured my mother's crumbly white dust into the lake, we were

Catharine Tipton (left front) and Alice, in her straw hat, pouring Miss Annie's ashes into the waters of Lake Martin off the dock of their family cabin; observing (from left to right) are Alice's second husband Rick LaFleur, her first husband Sam Whatley, her children Tipton and Sara Jane, and Catharine's husband Ken Sosebee; Uncle Dick Tipton watches from above, as his son, Cousin Rick, takes the snapshot.

well below the main dock, kneeling on the near edge of the connected floating platform. The water was shallow, clear and still. As we watched, her pale ashes made a small cloud, hitting the lake's dark bottom. Some of the family members were standing above us and everyone was very quiet as the cloud began to expand. It eventually formed a perfect halo and kept growing, never losing its shape until it had encircled us all. My children. My sister. Me. Our husbands. My cousins and Uncle Tip. The halo didn't begin to disperse and fade until it had reached out, 20 feet in diameter, to embrace us all.

Merged photos of Jim Tipton, my father and stubbornly modest hero, in Germany, early 1945, and Ann Little, my mother and intrepid swimmer, at Alouette, August, 1945.

ABOUT THE AUTHOR

Alice Ann Tipton LaFleur was born at Langley Air Force Base in Hampton, Virginia, on December 22, 1953, the younger daughter of General James Baird Tipton and Ann Livingston Little. As the children of an Air Force officer, she and her sister Catharine grew up all over the world—in Japan, Korea, and Turkey, and stateside in Virginia, Alabama, and Florida. As she moved around, Alice traveled widely in Europe, the Middle East, and throughout North America.

She earned degrees in both botany and plant pathology from Colorado State University and did graduate work in plant biochemistry at the University of Georgia. Alice and her first husband settled in Oglethorpe County, outside Athens, Georgia, where they raised two children, Sara Jane Whatley and Tipton James Whatley.

In 2005 she married Richard A. (Rick) LaFleur, a professor of Classics now retired from the University of Georgia. The two reside for most of the year in the home she designed for them on the banks of Lake Oglethorpe, and they spend several weeks each fall, winter, and spring at their cottages in Apalachicola, Florida, and Little Switzerland, North Carolina. Alice's foremost passions are her family, her gardens, and the local live music scene.

Alice with Rick, her editor and
encourager-in-chief